THE STORY OF

The Lone Ranger

Designed and edited by Hal Schuster

with James R. Martin

EDWARD GROSS has written for a variety of publications, including PREMIERE, STARLOG, COMICS SCENE, NEW YORK/LONG ISLAND NIGHTLIFE, FANGORIA and CINEFANTASTIQUE. He is the author of TREK: THE LOST YEARS, THE UNOFFICIAL TALE OF BEAUTY AND THE BEAST, THE MAKING OF THE NEXT GENERATION, THE ODD COUPLE COMPANION, SECRET FILE: THE MAKING OF A WISEGUY and PAUL McCARTNEY: 20 YEARS ON HIS OWN. In addition, he co-authored the story for an episode of ABC's SUPERCARRIER and his first screenplay is scheduled to go into production later this year. He lives on Long Island, New York with his wife Eileen and their son, Teddy.

THE STORY OF
The Lone Ranger

By James Van Hise

PIONEER BOOKS, INC.   LAS VEGAS, NEVADA

Library of Congress Cataloging-in-Publication Data
Edward Gross, 1960—

Who Was That Masked Man? The Story of the Lone Ranger

    1.   Who Was That Masked Man? The Story of the Lone Ranger (television)

 I. Title

Published by Pioneer Books, Inc., 5715 N. Balsam Rd., Las Vegas, NV, 89130.

First Printing, 1990

Dedicated to Clayton Moore

CONTENTS

Who Was That Masked Man?

There's something about a man in a mask. It made the Lone Ranger more than just an ordinary Western show however ordinary some of the plots might have been. When the hero is a man of mystery, it makes his adventures more exotic by extension. It was that mask which made the Lone Ranger stand out from the crowd even when he was a hero of the imagination experienced over the medium of audio entertainment which radio was in decades past. It's that mask! It made things even more interesting when the TV show had been on for several years and people would recognize him and not even question the fact that he was wearing a mask. When he'd soberly state that, "This mask is on the side of justice," one could only remark how strange it was to hear him say that. And unlike the world of super heroes where masked heroes and villains abounded, in the realm of the Lone Ranger, he was the *only* hero who wore a mask. Talking about individuality! And while other heroes such as Superman and Batman have recently passed their half-century mark with much hoopla, the Lone Ranger is three years away from his sixtieth birthday and remains a recognizable icon even though he currently is not appearing in comic books, comic strips, television or films except in TV reruns and on home video. Not bad for a character who's been in retirement since 1981. In fact, 1990-1991, will bring a John Landis-directed motion picture an d a new syndicated television series from Palladium Entertainment. The Lone Ranger is a character who captured the popular imagination in 1933 and has remained popular ever since, particularly in the memories of our youth, and those tend to be among our strongest recollections.

—-JAMES VAN HISE
January 1990

The Creation of a Legend

The creation of the Lone Ranger is a story in itself, one shrouded with the passage of time, obscured by the deaths of all principal players. That George W. Trendle, a canny businessman, created the character is without question. Yet decades after the fact Trendle was taking *sole* credit, something not really born out by the facts.

While success has many fathers and failure is an orphan, the Lone Ranger was a result of carefully crafted collaboration between businessman Trendle and the talent he hired to develop a show for his fledgling radio station, WXYZ. Trendle had a vision, but he needed creative people to breathe life into it.

Trendle was an entrepreneur in the truest sense of the word. In the Twenties he'd made millions from a chain of motion picture theaters. He sold the theaters in 1929 and managed to hold on to his millions while others lost theirs in the stock market crash and the dark years of the Great Depression. Trendle bought radio station WXYZ (formerly WGHP) in Detroit, a CBS affiliate, and entered another arena of entertainment—broadcasting. In 1932, Trendle wanted his station to keep the whole advertising revenue pie, rather than sharing ad time with

duced competed successfully on a local level, that was far from good enough. They needed something to market nationally.

One of Trendle's employees after he acquired the radio station was James Jewel, an all-around talent who wrote, acted and directed. Jewel was such a key player in the creation of the Lone Ranger that Trendle eventually made certain the man could not lay claim to the vast wealth generated by the property in the late Thirties, instead taking sole credit for the character.

James Jewell directed "The Lone

Ranger" radio series from its inception through 1938. He also directed "The Green Hornet" from its inception to 1938 and created "The Black Ace" radio show after leaving WXYZ. Jewell also wrote and directed many of the episodes of "Jack Armstrong, the All-American Boy" from 1943

CBS and paying them for the privilege of airing their shows. It proved a rash move, and one which he wasn't properly prepared for. Trendle found it difficult to fill all of the air time (18 hours per day) CBS had previously filled. It wasn't the same as putting on stage shows between features at the movie theaters he once owned. Radio drama was inexpensive to produce at that time. Trendle hired a band of performers who could do double or triple duty providing voices for characters on a variety of shows. Although the shows pro-

to 1951.

When Trendle worked on developing a thirty minute Western drama for his station to air, James Jewel fleshed out his ideas. During round table discussions of the character, James Jewell and station manager Harold True proposed and discarded the idea of naming the show The Lone Star Ranger because the name was already in use (but is long forgotten today). True then suggested the simpler "Lone Ranger" and the idea stuck. Jewell had been writing "The Manhunters" radio series for WXYZ and Trendle gave "The Lone Ranger" a late night un-announced try-out in either December 1932 or early January 1933 (reports vary as to the exact broadcast date). Fran Striker, the writer most identified with the radio show, arrived a few weeks later. Complicating this scenario is the original manuscript to Striker's first Lone Ranger script in the archives at the State University of New York at Buffalo. On the cover sheet, it says at the top:

THE LONE RANGER
NUMBER 1
4 MEN 1 WOMAN.

But below the description of the number of actors needed is the hand-written notation "Dec. 1932." That this was probably a false clue added later by Striker or someone else can be determined by the fact that even though the script says NUMBER 1, it is not the first "Lone Ranger" script ever done, just the first one written by Striker. It may well have been the first one broadcast after earlier drafts were rejected. Although there was a question as to whether the Lone Ranger started out with a mask, Striker's first script clearly states: "Thruout (sic) the entire West, in those turbulent days, were circulated stories of a masked rider, a picturesque figure that performed deeds of the greatest daring. A modern Robin Hood. . . seen by few, known by none. Whence he came and where he went, no one ever knew. Few men had dared to defy this LONE RANGER, and those that had, were found dead. The daring adventures of the Lone Ranger, the mystery rider, will be presented in this new series of programs." This is very different from the later, more pristine, version of the Lone Ranger who would only shoot to wound.

Fran Striker lived in Buffalo writing scripts for a number of radio stations and selling them first broadcast rights based on the size of the station. WXYZ was a 1,000 watt station so Striker agreed to write scripts for them at four dollars per half hour. His first Lone Ranger scripts were recycled from "Covered Wagon Days," a Western series he'd been writing for airing in Buffalo. The Lone Ranger doesn't even appear in the first several pages of the first script as a prospector tells his wife stories he'd just heard about the mystery man known as The Lone Ranger.

Lone Ranger badges and buttons were issued in numberous shapes and sizes based on various themes throughout the Thirties and Forties—today they are highly collectible premiums.

Inspiration for The Lone Ranger came by way of such characters as Robin Hood and Zorro. The try-out script had the Ranger laughing as he rode off, but then the actor couldn't do the laugh convincingly. Director James Jewell worked with George Seaton, the first actor to portray the Lone Ranger. Looking for something more convincing than Seaton's laugh, "Hi-Yo Silver" was born. That it would become the signature of the character wasn't even considered in those stressful moments shortly before air time.

The Lone Ranger has been featured in serials, movies, radio drama, comic books and on television.

As The Lone Ranger was in it's early trial days of on-air development, Tonto joined around the fourth show as it was difficult writing a story in which the main character could only communicate twists in the story by telling his horse. Although "The Lone Ranger" had a narrator (early on this was Brace Beemer, who would take over the job of The Lone Ranger in 1941), a story could not be told with narration alone, but with lots of interaction between characters.

Examining radio scripts, one is struck by how similar they are to movie and television scripts. They contain dialogue and stage directions, but instead of camera moves the stage directions guide the use of sound effects vital in making the story sound real and alive. Radio drama is the theatre of the mind and can inspire the imagination in vital ways, much like reading can. Radio has the advantage of a sense of immediacy and reality enhanced by the use of sound effects. These techniques may be of secondary importance in motion pictures, but in radio, they reign supreme.

James Jewell, the first director of "The Lone Ranger," remained an important figure in the genesis of the character because Fran Striker chose to stay in Buffalo, New York. Striker mailed his scripts in until November 1934 when he finally relocated to Detroit due to the continuing and increasing demands of his work for Trendle. If one of Striker's scripts was late arriving by mail, Jewell sat down to pound out a rapidly needed substitute.

Who was recognized as creating the character became more important to Trendle as the value of the copyright increased. Harold True, having come up with the name, felt he deserved a piece of the action. But since True was an employee of Trendle's, ownership of an idea created for his employer as part of his job was not allowed. True couldn't secure anything legally, and an attorney told him so. Yet Trendle was so concerned he did a remarkable thing in 1938— he tricked James Jewell into signing away all future claims on the character. Trendle regarded contracts as important only so long as they were favorable to him. Jewell's first contract with Trendle paid $25 a script. When Trendle discovered this was far above average, he broke the contract and forced Jewell to accept less. This should have tipped Jewell off as to what kind of businessman Trendle could be, but Trendle still talked Jewell into accepting a compromise.

Jewell was very involved in the early creative years of the Lone Ranger and even decades later was able to prove that "kemo sabe" was his addition to the lore. "Kee Mo Sah Bee" was the name of a summer camp owned by Jewell's father-in-law and established in 1911 at Mullet Lake, Michigan. He picked up the word "tonto,"

A GIANT COMIC

25¢

the Lone Ranger

MOVIE STORY *plus*

1. ALL ABOUT THE LONE RANGER
2. TONTO'S EARLY LIFE
3. SILVER IN WILD HORSE VALLEY

meaning "wild one," from Indians who lived near the camp. Being the only two Indian words he remembered, he incorporated them into the show. This was revealed in an interview conducted with author David Rothel some months before Jewell's death.

Trendle foresaw the value of his property in 1933. The station owner told James Jewell he wanted him to sign an assignment of authorship. Upon securing legal advice, Jewell agreed to do so for a ten percent interest in the character. Trendle talked him out of this and said he'd think about five percent if Jewell signed. Trusting his boss, Jewell did and later, when asked about the five percent, Trendle said he had no idea what Jewell was talking about. Jewell quit WXYZ in 1938 when Brace Beemer rejoined the station's staff and became his boss. Jewell had never gotten along with the egotistical Beemer when he'd been the announcer for "The Lone Ranger" for a time in 1933 and had no interest in working under the man.

Frank Striker had an agreement which paid him $10 a show more for every new station signed up to carry the Lone Ranger. Trendle one day told Striker he'd decided to just give him an across the board $50 a week raise in place of the old agreement. Striker agreed and a week later Trendle announced that 120 new stations had signed up to carry the Lone Ranger, which made that $50 raise pale into insignificance. Yet Striker remained with the Lone Ranger and WXYZ and eventually shared in the profits.

Striker wrote three episodes of the Lone Ranger each week as well as much of the merchandising tie-in material and by 1950 was earning $50,000 a year, a great deal of money in those days. Striker felt rewarded and publicly linked his name with the character far more than Trendle's was, although Trendle's ownership of the title was secure. The radio show remained on the air until September 3, 1954 when the 2,956th episode was broadcast, and Fran Striker remained with the series until the end as the head writer.

The first Lone Ranger on radio was George Seaton, who later went on to become a film director. After a few months he was replaced by Earle W. Graser, who was so popular in the role that when he died in an auto accident in April 1941 at the age of 32, there were hundreds of people who turned out for his funeral who had never met him. They all had heard his familiar voice from the radio three nights a week for several years.

Brace Beemer, who had been the announcer for "The Lone Ranger" since the late Thirties, stepped into the role. Although Beemer had a deep bass voice, it was by no means indistinguishable from Graser's. So a story unfolded in which the Lone Ranger was injured and over a couple episodes regained his voice, only slightly altered. Beemer remained in the role of radio's Lone Ranger until the end of the show in 1954. Although some sources indicate Beemer played the Lone Ranger on radio in the early Thirties, James Jewell, the director of the radio show from 1933 through 1938, disputed this. The confusion may have arisen because when WXYZ needed a Lone Ranger for personal appearances in the early Thirties, Brace Beemer was selected to don the mask because he fit the likeness of the character and was an experienced horseman. Beemer trimmed down and tried out for the part in 1949 when television cast for the role, but with no film experience to his credit, he was turned down for the demanding job of starring in a weekly TV series.

On radio, Tonto was played by John Todd, an older actor who remained with the radio show until its conclusion in 1954 when he was 77. He wasn't an Indian. On radio, the sound of your voice mattered, not your physical attributes. Todd died at the age of 80 in 1957.

Most everyone once involved with the Lone Ranger radio show have now passed on. George Seaton, who became best known for directing the perennial classic MIRACLE ON 34th STREET, died in 1979 at the age of 68. Brace Beemer died in 1965 at the age of 62. Fran Striker died in Buffalo, New York in an auto accident in 1962 at the age of 59. James Jewell died in 1975, and George W. Trendle passed away in 1972 at the ripe old age of 87. Fred Foy is still alive, and although he's the best-known announcer from both the radio and the television series, he didn't begin working on the radio program until 1947. All the principal players in the creation of the Lone Ranger are now gone, and we must depend on published records and interviews to piece together the story. That Trendle's own autobiography is unreliable is widely known; James Jewell isn't even mentioned in reference to the Lone Ranger even though he was the show's first director for five years and wrote fill-in scripts when necessary. Like the character himself, the origin of the Lone Ranger will become more

deeply enshrouded in legend as time goes on.

In fact, 1990-1991, will bring a John Landis-directed motion picture an d a new syndicated television series from Palladium Entertainment.

TYPICAL MOVIE PROMOTIONAL ITEMS FOR THE SERIAL THE LONE RANGER SELLS FOR $75 to $250.

The Lone Ranger

Shrouded almost as darkly in legend as the Lone Ranger himself, this serial was considered lost for many years and to this day has still not been completely restored. While one would think the first appearance of the Lone Ranger on the screen would be a classic film carefully protected by the copyright holders, the owners of the Lone Ranger today have no idea what happened to it. Or why the original negative of the chapter-play is nowhere to be found. What did happen is a Hollywood story in the truest sense of the word.

Although William Witney once tld a convention audience that THE LONE RANGER cost a "million dollars" to make, the files at Republic Studios reveal the actual cost was $168,315, which was only $8,000 over budget. The complicated story delivered a far better than average serial, and its sequel, THE LONE RANGER RIDES AGAIN (1939), suffers badly by comparison.

After a lonely start on radio station WXYZ in January of 1933, the Lone Ranger rode to fame, heard three times a week nationwide by January of 1937. Re-

public was notified in February of 1937 that the Lone Ranger was available as a motion picture property. It was actually first considered for, and then rejected as, a vehicle for a Gene Autry. Only then was it considered for a serial.

Trendle protected his character, and although Republic was notorious for exercising strict control over screenplays and reserving the final say on scripts, Trendle included restrictions in the contract as to how the Lone Ranger, Tonto and Silver could be portrayed. The Lone Ranger was to be at least

five feet eleven inches, carry 170 pounds, wear a white hat, be clean-shaven and not swear. Tonto was to be shorter than the Lone Ranger. Silver must be a white stallion. This image of the Lone Ranger and Tonto made it to the screen and became the image of the characters for decades to come.

The only item that ever changed was the mask. The radio show never stipulated exactly what kind of mask the Ranger wore and Trendle neglected to stipulate this in the contract he signed with Republic.

Republic paid Trendle $18,750 for the rights to make THE LONE RANGER as a serial, and promised to pay an additional 10% royalty on whatever rentals the serial returned above $390,000. "Rentals" refers to the dollar amount returned to the studio as their share of the ticket price paid by patrons for admission to a theater to see a motion picture. Trendle provided Republic with 66 of Fran Striker's radio scripts as story reference and the studio drafted a screenplay in which the Lone Ranger's identity remained a secret until the final episode. Trendle hadn't considered that Republic would abandon the masked mystery man aspect of the Lone Ranger and argued against it to no avail.

The serial portrayed the origin of the Lone Ranger much as it had been described on the radio show, but the often used motif of "six Texas Rangers" became a more realistic twenty for the serial, making it easier for a single survivor to be overlooked by the raiders. Butch Cavendish was also nowhere to be seen, and the aspect of one of the slain Rangers being the Lone Ranger's brother was also abandoned. Tonto still found the survivor and nursed him back to health, but the name given in the serial turned out to be "Allen King," not any form of Reid as he would eventually be known through the radio shows and later films and television shows. For no discernable reason, Republic gave the Ranger a completely different secret identity in THE LONE RANGER RIDES AGAIN, that of "Bill Andrews." Also different from the traditional origin was having the Lone Ranger be one of five mystery heroes, as he would switch from his civilian identity to the Lone Ranger whenever the need arose, not unlike Zorro. But even though Zorro had been one of the inspirations for the Lone Ranger, one of the things which set the masked rider of the plains apart from other masked heroes is that he had no life other than being the Lone Ranger. He wasn't one person by day and the Lone Ranger by night. The serial ignored this, opting for the traditional approach to the masked do-gooder established by other characters, including Republic's own version of Zorro in 1937's ZORRO RIDES AGAIN, from whom the unusual full-face mask was borrowed.

The serial establishes early on that one of five Texans is the Lone Ranger. They are rounded up and put in a cell as one of Smith's henchmen has determined that the Lone Ranger must be one of these men. How he arrived at this de-termination is never made clear, but he was right. Once the men are locked in the same cell and left alone, we see one of them, masked by shadows, admit, "I am the Lone Ranger." The others then agree to help him, although the audience is still unaware of which of the heroes the masked man really is. Thus for fifteen

OPPOSITE: Allen King and Tonto. Is it the Lone Ranger or isn't it? Watch the gun belt!

chapters, as the other Rangers are gradually killed off one-by-one, we can try to guess which one he is. Even knowing it's Lee Powell there are no honest clues to tip us off.

Further complicating matters, whenever the Lone Ranger donned his full face mask, his voice deepened, dubbed by actor Billy Bletcher. Although Bletcher never portrayed the masked man on the radio, his voice was similar, and Republic's choice showed they were very aware of the distinctive bass tones identified with the Lone Ranger.

Besides THE LONE RANGER, Lee Powell also starred in FIGHTING DEVIL DOGS (Republic, 1938) and co-starred in FLASH GORDON CONQUERS THE UNIVERSE (Universal, 1940). In 1939 he made some personal appearances as the Lone Ranger until forced to stop by Trendle and

Republic, as Powell was no longer under contract to Republic at the time. He made a few Westerns after this, and then enlisted in the Marine Corps in World War Two, meeting his end in action on the island of Tinian in the Pacific on July 29, 1944. When he died, he was only 36. Some have suggested that had Powell survived and continued in serials, he might have been a bigger star than Buster Crabbe. But such is the way of life.

Complicating the guessing game, the Ranger was played by stunt man Yakima Canutt in fights and action sequences. At Houstoncon '73, director William Witney told the following anecdote about Canutt: "There's a funny story about Yak on THE LONE RANGER. They had that mask that came down to here (indicating the screen on the bottom half of the mask) and Yak always chewed to-

bacco. Now, he wore that mask so much that he'd forget it was there and all of a sudden you'd hear him say, 'Dammit!' and you knew what happened—he'd spit into the mask."

Today, the only versions of THE LONE RANGER and THE LONE RANGER RIDES AGAIN which exist are Mexican prints with Spanish subtitles. Worse, THE LONE RANGER was incomplete in the Mexican print and the only versions of chapters 10 and 15 that could be located are dubbed into French with the English track completely replaced except for the trademark cry of "Hi-Yo Silver!" These are available on video in varying quality. In the serial, when Tonto is shown in the opening credits, rather than giving his stage name (Chief Thunder Cloud, which appears in a later block of credits), he's listed as "Tonto." In the Mexican print, because "Ton-

to" means fool in Spanish, he's called "Ponto," but his name is not re-dubbed in the film's sound track. The subtitles keep calling him Ponto instead of Tonto.

Chief Thunder Cloud's non-Indian name was Victor Daniels, although this isn't reflected in any of the film's credits. He was born in 1900 and died in 1955. His other film credits include RAMONA (1936), RENFREW OF THE ROYAL MOUNTED (1937), GERONIMO (1939), TYPHOON (1940), NORTHWEST MOUNTED POLICE (1941) BUFFALO BILL (1944), THE SENATOR WAS INDESCREET (1947), AMBUSH (1949), DAVY CROCKETT INDIAN SCOUT (1950) and others.

Although one story circulating states that Republic had to destroy the prints and original negatives due to a copyright infringement action launched by Trendle, records in Republic's files don't back this up. The facts are more arcane. Herb Yates (1880-1966), the head of Republic, was pleased with the performance of the Lone Ranger serial and wanted to make a third, but discovered on the eve of the release of THE LONE RANGER RIDES AGAIN that Universal had both The Lone Ranger and The Green Hornet in development, and that one of the writers on Republic's serials, Barry Shipman, was working on the drafts for Universal. Yates entered into protracted talks with Trendle and his representatives, and this time Trendle demanded the Lone Ranger not be unmasked. Trendle

also increased his asking price to $50,000 plus 10% of the world-wide gross as opposed to a percentage of net profits as on the

OPPOSITE:
Joan Blanchard takes center stage while, in the background, Tonto watches over. Rangers (L. to R.): Bob Stuart, Bert Rogers, Jim Clark, Dick Forrest and Allen King

first serial. They all but settled on $45,000 but Republic wanted 12 to 18 months after the serial was released to put out a feature version. This Trendle refused as their agreement allowed him to offer a fourth serial to any interested party and he felt this would delay him too long. By the time the agreement with Republic finally unravelled, Universal had also lost interest in doing a Lone Ranger serial. They did go on to make two Green Hornet serials from another property owned by Trendle.

Herb Yates, as President of Republic, felt Westerns were a dime a dozen and didn't like being held up for rights. When the negotiations fell apart, he had all original negatives and prints destroyed. Yates often let his temper get the better of him. He was married to former ice skating star Vera Hruba Ralston, whom he made a star at Republic even though she was not a very good actress. In 1949 the studio's biggest star, John Wayne, went to Yates and insisted he didn't want to work with her in any more films. This infuriated Yates. Wayne only made one more film at Republic after that, THE QUIET MAN in 1952.

THE LONE RANGER was released as a feature version, under the title HI-YO SILVER!, in 1940. And that was Republic's last brush with the masked man. Reportedly Yates tried to negotiate with Trendle again briefly several years later, in 1947, when the rights were offered for television, but the talks never went anywhere.

The copyright on the Lone Ranger has changed hands twice since Republic made those two serials and today the owner has no idea what happened to the serials nor why they don't have access to the potentially valuable negatives or positive prints of the first celluloid versions of the character. By 1956, the serials had been forgotten by the then-current copyright holder, Jack Wrather Productions. When the June 30, 1956 issue of TV GUIDE ran an article on the Lone Ranger and showed photos of the previous actors who'd played the character, the radio performers were pictured along with the two TV Rangers, John Hart and Clayton Moore. The serials weren't mentioned nor did photos of Lee Powell and Robert Livingston appear in the article, which claimed that five actors had played the part to date, rather than the seven.

The film of THE LONE RANGER (1938) which exists today is far from perfect, but it is in good enough condition to be watched. We can still see that it was not only one of Republic's best Western serials, but one of its best overall. Whether a complete English language print will ever be found, much less one in pristine condition, remains problematic at best. When the Lone Ranger rode off into the sunset at the end of that serial, he almost rode off once and for all!

The Lone Ranger

DIRECTORS: William Witney
and John English
SCREEN PLAY: Barry Shipman,
George Worthington Yates,
Franklyn Adreon,
Ronald Davidson and Lois Eby
ASSOCIATE PRODUCER:
Sol C. Siegel
SUPERVISED BY: Robert Beche
PRODUCTION MANAGER:
Al Wilson
UNIT MANAGER:
Mack D'Agostino
PHOTOGRAPHY:
William Nobles
FILM EDITORS: Helen Turner
and Edward Todd
MUSICAL DIRECTOR:
Alberto Colombo
RELEASE DATE: March 4, 1938

CAST
THE LONE RANGER:
Lee Powell
LONE RANGER'S VOICE:
Bill Bletcher
SILVER: Silver Chief
TONTO: Chief Thunder Cloud
JOAN BLANCHARD:
Lynn Roberts
MARK SMITH: Stanley Andrews
GEORGE BLANCHARD:
George Cleveland
FATHER McKIM:
William Farnum
ALLEN KING: Lee Powell
BERT ROGERS: Herman Brix
DICK FORREST: Lane Chandler
BOB STUART: Hal Taliaferro
SAMMY: Sammy McKim
IKE LEWIN: Yakima Canutt
KESTER: John Merton
JIM CLARK: George Letz
BLACK TAGGART:
Raphael Bennett
FELTON: Tom London
JOE SNEAD: Maston Williams

BLAKE: Charles Thomas
BRENNAN: Allan Cavan
BROWN: Reed Howes
JOE CANNON: Walter James
CARPETBAGGER:
Francis Sayles
MATT CLARK:
Murdock McQuarrie
MRS. CLARK: Jane Keckley
DARK CLOUD: Phillip Armenta
DRAKE: Ted Adams
GUARD: Jimmy Hollywood
GUNMAN ONE: Jack Kirk
GUNMAN TWO: Art Dillard
GUNMAN THREE:
Millard McGowan
GUNMAN FOUR: Frank Ellis
HASKINS: Carl Stockdale
HOBART: Bud Osborne
HOLT: Fred Burns
INDIAN WOMAN: Inez Cody
JAILER: Duke Green
MARCUS JEFFRIES:
Forbes Murray
MARINA: Edna Lawrence
MORELY: Charles King
MORGAN: Jack Perrin
PEDRO: Frank Leyva
PEPITO: George Mari
PERKINS: Charles Whitaker
RANCE: Edmund Cobb
REGAN: Jack Rockwell
RUNNING ELK: J.W. Cody
SENTRY ONE: Carl Saxe
SENTRY TWO: George Magrill
WHITE FEATHER:
Iron Eyes Cody

EPISODE ONE: "HEIGH-YO SILVER!"

The setting is Texas, after the Civil War. A band of outlaws, led by Mark Smith, turns to banditry in order to increase its fortunes. In a raid on a wagon train, they capture a functionary of the Federal Government, one Col. Jeffries, who has been sent to set up the Tax Commission in Texas. Sensing an opportunity to gain power,

Smith disposes of Jeffries and assumes both his identity and the position of Commissioner of Finances, using the Federal documents as his guarantee.

"Jeffries" then begins to take over the state, abusing his usurped power for his own ends. The Texas Rangers, led by Captain Rance, head in towards Pecos when they learn of these abuses, but are ambushed by Jeffries troopers and the cowardly Joe Snead. Trapped in a box canyon, subjected to gunfire from above, they fight valiantly but are soon wiped out.

Under cover of night, the solitary Indian, Tonto, searches the battlefield, but finds only one survivor. He takes the wounded man back to a hidden cave and nurses him back to health. His head bandaged, his face unseen, the survivor is informed that he is the only man to have lived. At this news, he

swears a solemn oath in his deep, resonant voice:

"The only one... the Lone Ranger. I'll never rest until these deaths are avenged!"

Soon, the Lone Ranger appears to rouse the people against Jeffries. His face is obscured by his hat, and by a mask which covers his face, leaving only his eyes uncovered, unlike the smaller mask favored by later versions of the Ranger. Riding through the land around Pecos, he urges the oppressed ranchers to join him at the old adobe stockade in the San Juan Valley, and all join him gladly.

Meanwhile, Jeffries has learned that a special Federal administer, Blanchard, has been sent from Washington. His most pressing concern is to keep Blanchard in the dark. He sends Joe Snead to infiltrate the stockade. Snead already suspects that the Lone Rang-

This scene never appeared in the serial.

er is one of five men, and so he entraps these five on a mission to raise food and ammo for the ranchers.

The five are imprisoned. Jeffries gives the Lone Ranger fifteen minutes to reveal himself, promising to spare the others in return for his confession. In the darkened cell, he reveals himself to his friends, but they swear to stick together despite all adversity. Snead overhears this, but cannot see which man is the Ranger. He could be Jim Clark, Burt Rogers, Dick Forrest, Allen King, or Bob Stewart. Jeffries hedges his bets by ar-

ranging for the immediate execution of all five.

Snead heads for the stockade, followed by a party of troopers, while a firing squad is assembled. The execution is interrupted by the arrival of Blanchard and his daughter, in a coach drawn by six horses. Tonto, always close at hand, steals the carriage, providing the five rangers and himself with a means of escape. Troopers pursue them across the plain, as the rangers leapfrog from horse to horse. At last only Tonto remains on the carriage, leaping to safety only aft-

er he has set it loose to block a narrow pass and cut off their pursuers.

They pause to change horses. The Lone Ranger dons his disguise, and he and Tonto race toward the stockade. Snead is already there. All the ranchers except the sentry are in the meeting hall, and Snead, his treachery unknown, gains entrance easily. The sentry falls, struck from behind, but Snead cannot find the key to the gate, and must resort to gunpowder to let the troopers in.

The Ranger, noticing the lack of a sentry, scales the palisade with a rope. He and Snead fight as the fuse grows ever shorter, until the gate explodes. The Ranger attempts to repel the attacking troopers, but there are too many, and he is only able to pick off half a dozen or so with his six-guns before they ride through the gate, knocking him to the ground.

CHAPTER TWO: "THUNDERING EARTH!"

The conclusion of chapter one proves to be a bit of a cheat, after all. The race to the stockade and the fist-fight with Snead are recapitulated without alteration, but the explosion is shown to have roused the ranchers from their meeting. They rush out to join the Ranger at the gate, barricade the opening with a cart, and repel the troopers after a lengthy gunfight. Not one trooper passes through the gate, and the Lone Ranger stands his ground. Snead does not appear again, having died in the explosion.

On their way back to Pecos, the routed troopers encounter Tonto, recognize him as "the Lone Ranger's Indian," and take off in pursuit. Tonto's horse falls beneath him, only to get up and ride off alone after Tonto is captured. The troopers try to elicit information about the Lone Ranger, but Tonto refuses, prompting Captain Kester to observe, "There are ways of making anyone talk."

Meanwhile, the Lone Ranger encounters Tonto's horse, which, being almost as smart as Silver, leads him to the place where Tonto is being whipped. The Ranger gets the drop on the troopers, disarms them, and has Tonto keep them covered while he engaged in a fistfight with Kester. He gives this scoundrel a sound drubbing, and leaves him with a parting thought: "Now maybe you'll think twice before using a whip!"

In Pecos, the priest Father McKim passes Blanchard a note which reads:

"Ask Col. Jeffries who massacred the Rangers at Grant's Pass."

Blanchard confronts Jeffries, places him under arrest, and heads for the stockade to tell the ranchers that they can return home. Once he is gone, Jeffries is unperturbed, for when the ranchers leave the stockade they will fall easy prey to the troopers. The ranchers believe Blanchard's promises of justice, and follow his advice, not knowing that an ambush is being set up. Tonto observes all this and rushes for the Lone Ranger's hideout.

Blanchard and the ranchers head

out, and are attacked by a party of troopers whose goal is to drive them towards a gorge where more troopers have set enough gunpowder to trigger an avalanche. The Lone Ranger arrives just in time to engage in another fist-fight as a fuse grows shorter, culminating in another explosion which causes a spectacular avalanche and knocks him to the ground.

CHAPTER THREE: "THE PIT-FALL"

As boulders thunder into the pass, stopping the progress of the wagon train, the Lone Ranger gets back up on his feet, but is unable to prevent Jeffries' men from capturing Blanchard and his daughter, Joan. The Ranger advises the ranchers to cross the border to safety.

Back in Pecos, Jeffries informs Blanchard of Lincoln's assassination. He threatens Joan and forces Blanchard to declare him Magistrate with regard to Federal affairs. When ;this is made public, the people believe that Blanchard has sold them out. Jeffries encour-

ages this by arranging for Joan to accompany him in public. On one of these occasions, the Ranger tosses a note to Joan, and she visits Father McKim's chapel to meet him. She tells him that her father is being forced to send Washington a letter recommending that Jeffries be appointed Governor-General of the state. When she learns when it will be sent, she will signal from her window.

Later, she eavesdrops as Jeffries dictates the letter to Blanchard. Blanchard signs, but Jeffries has to remind him to stamp it with his official seal; otherwise, the letter will not be valid. Joan learns that the letter goes out the next morning, and signals the news. She is discovered, but not before the Lone Ranger sees her signal.

The next morning, she escapes from under guard by disguising herself as her maid. Tonto and the Lone Ranger prepare to intercept the letter, while troopers prepare a trap for them: a pitfall, filled with sharp wooden stakes and covered with canvas, will lie right in their path. Fortunately, they see it being dug, and plan to avoid it.

They intercept the messenger and another rider, only to hear the approaching hoofbeats of another horse. The Ranger lies in wait, gun at the ready, realizing only at the last minute that the rider is Joan. She passes him, headed straight for the deadly pitfall. He mounts Silver and pursues her, but both riders fall, and seem destined to

plunge into the trap as the episode ends.

CHAPTER FOUR: "AGENTS OF TREACHERY"

The Lone Ranger is revealed to be clinging to the edge of the pit, while Joan lies, unharmed, some distance short of it. He climbs out, and they make good their escape while Tonto lays down covering fire. The letter is destroyed. Joan refuses to go to a safe place, for her father will be killed if she does not return. She tells the Ranger that another letter will be written, but that it would be unofficial without the seal.

That night, just as Blanchard is about to sign and seal a second letter, the lights go out. When order is restored, the seal is gone, and in its place are two silver bullets.

Jeffries plots against the Lone Ranger, and enlists the aid of Black Taggart, a condemned outlaw. The Ranger (without his costume) and his men are set up to believe that Black Taggart is being tortured by the troopers, and so they rescue him in good faith. Taggart claims to have papers that will incriminate Jeffries, and promises to turn them over to the Lone Ranger at a cabin in Eagle Gulch.

The Ranger walks into the set up. Two troopers lie in wait. He deals with them easily enough, but has a lengthy fist-fight with Black Taggart. Taggart seems to gain the upper hand through treachery. More troopers arrive just in time to see a masked man stagger out the cabin door. They unmask him, only to discover Black Taggart! The Ranger, in Taggart's clothes, his face concealed by a kerchief, steps out, six-guns drawn. All the troopers drop their guns, except one concealed behind their horses. He draws his gun, then reconsiders, picks up a large rock, and throws it at the Lone Ranger. The Ranger is struck on the head, and collapses.

CHAPTER FIVE: "THE STEAMING CAULDRON"

The Ranger is down, but Tonto arrives in the nick of time, guns blazing. The Ranger pulls himself together, and they escape, eluding the pursuing troopers by hiding behind a boulder.

Taggart returns to Pecos under guard. Joan, seeing him in the Ranger's clothes, passes him a note. Taggart uses this information to catch Father McKim in the act of sending a carrier pigeon message to the real Ranger, and substitutes his own message. The note tells the Ranger that Blanchard and Joan can escape if he will meet them at the mill.

Taggart informs Jeffries of this ploy, but Jeffries is not pleased, for the mill just happens to be the location of his secret cache of ammunition. The troopers arrive after the rangers, and gunshots are exchanged, but the troopers retreat

for fear of exploding the powder. The rangers escape from the mill by rolling lit powder kegs out the door into the path of the troopers.

As the escape is made, Taggart shoots one of the rangers, and follows him to the cave. The wounded man is Jim Clark. Taggart asks Clark if he is the Lone Ranger. "Sure," says Clark, "I'm the Lone Ranger." Taggart steps back to shoot Clark, but his gun is suddenly shot out of his hand by the real Lone Ranger.

Taggart and the Ranger engage in another lengthy fist-fight, which leads them ever deeper into the steaming, sulphurous depths of the cave. Taggart falls into a crevice, landing on the narrow edge of a bubbling, steaming pit, and calls to his enemy for help.

"You deserve no better," says the Ranger, "but I'll help you." The treacherous Taggart turns the table

on the generous hero, leaving him trapped in his stead.

CHAPTER SIX: "RED MAN'S COURAGE"

Taggart tries to leave, but Silver rears up and attacks him, and he falls directly into one of the volcanic pits to his well-deserved fate. The Lone Ranger, unable to lasso any of the crumbling rocks lining the rim of his trap, calls Silver and throws his rope over the pommel of the faithful steed's saddle, and makes good his escape. He rushes to Jim Clark's side, only to witness his dying breath.

The four remaining rangers hold a funeral for Clark, and Tonto sings to the sunset in his memory.

Jeffries, meanwhile, ponders the possibility of using Indians to track the Lone Ranger. Kester informs him that all the Indians are friends with the Ranger. The villains decide to change this situation. They hire Perkins and Blake, a pair of good-for-nothings, to help them. Perkins and Blake shoot two Comanche braves in the back and leave two silver bullets (left behind by the Ranger in Chapter Four) at the scene of the crime. Chief Dark Cloud concludes, from this evidence, that the Lone Ranger has turned against them.

The Comanches capture Tonto, who refuses to tell them the Ranger's whereabouts. They prepare to burn him at the stake. The Ranger learns of Tonto's abduction and races to the Comanche camp, only to plummet from his saddle upon his arrival. The flames grow higher about Tonto as the episode ends.

CHAPTER SEVEN: "WHEELS OF DISASTER"

The Lone Ranger gets up and kicks out the fire before he is restrained by the Comanche warriors. Chief Dark Cloud accuses the

kins dead, and expires from his own wounds.

The Ranger, Tonto and the Comanches renew their friendship with the peace pipe ritual.

His latest plan foiled, Jeffries decides to move the rest of his ammunition out of the mill. Tonto observes the troopers carrying out these orders. The four rangers ride out and capture some ammunition. To prevent this from happening again, Jeffries puts Joan Blanchard on the next powder wagon.

Tonto must now race to stop the ranchers who are riding out to capture or destroy the gunpowder,

Ranger of murdering two braves, and cites the silver bullets as proof. The Ranger asks if any silver bullets were actually found in the bodies. A brave rushes into a tent and returns a moment later with the news: the victims were killed with ordinary bullets. The Ranger and Tonto are cleared.

As this is going on, Perkins and Blake sneak up on the Indian camp. Silver attacks Blake with his hooves, wounding him severely, and Perkins is captured. Perkins tries to pin both killings on Blake. Blake, enraged, shoots Per-

while the Ranger hides on the back of the wagon.

The ranchers see that the wagon is heavily guarded, and decide to fire a volley to explode the gunpowder. The Ranger tosses a lit powder keg off the back of the wagon, separating the troopers from it, and engages in a long fight with the driver of the wagon. In a reprise of the famous "Stagecoach" stunt created by Yakima Canutt (this could be Canutt in this scene), the Lone Ranger is dragged under the horses, then the carriage, only to climb up over the back of the wagon and subdue his opponent. He regains control of the wagon, but only briefly, for a bullet hits the powder and the wagon explodes.

CHAPTER EIGHT: "FATAL TREASURE"

Joan is revealed to have moved off the wagon and onto one of the horses. The harness has been separated from the wagon by the explosion, and the Ranger has fallen off, unharmed. He is unable to keep her from being recaptured by the troopers.

Back in Pecos, Jeffries awaits the arrival of a contingent of Federal Cavalry, led by Lieutenant Brown. Brown's mission is to take charge of the silver money "Jeffries" has collected as taxes. Jeffries intends to keep the silver and hand over worthless Confederate paper mon-

without arousing Federal suspicion. Joan overhears his plans, and sends a message to the Ranger with one of Father McKim's pigeons.

That night, the Ranger steals the silver for safekeeping, and hides it in the well. In the morning, the four rangers sneak into town disguised as water carriers. Two of them lower themselves into the well and load the silver in the water barrels carried by their donkeys. At the conclusion of their task they prepare to depart, but must leave the two men in the well behind due to the arrival of some troopers. A thirsty trooper commandeers one of the water barrels; they leave it behind so as not to arouse suspicion, and make their escape. Another trooper sees that the water barrel is in the sun, and tries to move the barrel into the shade, only to find it too heavy to move. He is astonished to find sil-

ver coins at the bottom of the barrel. The troopers are alerted just as the two rangers in the well try to climb out. The two parties exchange fire briefly, until Kester brings a cannon to bear on the well, and destroys it.

CHAPTER NINE: "THE MISSING SPUR"

ey, under the pretext that this is the only money the ranchers have. This plan is foiled when Lt. Brown arrives earlier than expected, and sees the silver in Jeffries office. Now Jeffries must plot to steal the silver from the bank

The well destroyed by Kester's cannon is only one of a number of wells over the cistern. The two rangers climb out of another well, behind the troopers, and capture

Kester as a guarantee of their safety. Once they are out of sight of Pecos, they set him free to walk back to town.

Jeffries sends his men out to stop the rangers from getting the silver to the Federal troops at Fort Bentley. Tonto hears their approach by clamping his teeth around the branch of a tree and feeling the vibrations of nearing hoofbeats sent up from the deep roots of the tree. Tonto then takes the silver to a safe place while the rangers draw the troopers in another direction. Federal cavalry intercedes in their battle, capture the rangers and take them to Ft. Bentley.

Kester wants Lt. Brown to hand the rangers over to him, but they are charged with stealing tax money, a Federal offense, and must be tried in Federal court in Ft. Bentley. Furthermore, the rangers tell Brown that the silver will be handed over to the proper authorities.

Tonto switches clothes with a Mexican porter and takes the rangers their food. The Lone Ranger slips into the poncho and sombrero and escapes, to bring the silver to the fort. As he does so, Kester grapples with him briefly, and manages to grab one of his spurs before he rides off. The silver has been turned over to the Federal government, and Jeffries' plan has been foiled.

Kester is certain to learn who the Lone Ranger is, since he can only be whichever ranger escaped from their cell. But when he and Brown in-

vestigate, all four men are still there. Kester isn't through yet, though. Whichever man is wearing only one spur is certain to be the Ranger. The episode ends as Kester looks up from the boots of the one-spurred man and exclaims, "The Lone Ranger!"

CHAPTER TEN: "FLAMING FURY"

The other three men then step forward. All of them have only one spur! The Lone Ranger's identity remains a secret.

The next day, Kester plans to take charge of the rangers, who are under his jurisdiction now that the Federal charges against them have been dropped. But they have already escaped their cell, leaving a single spur and four silver bullets behind.

Meanwhile, Jeffries plans to improve his public image by marrying Joan. She hates him, but agrees to the marriage to save her father's life. Another pigeon message, by way of Father McKim, alerts the Lone Ranger, who races to stop the ceremony. Jeffries has already spoken his vows before

the Ranger arrives, and Joan hesitates just long enough to allow the Ranger to disrupt the proceedings. Enraged by Jeffries' disregard for womanhood, the Ranger beats him with a horsewhip, and promises to finish him off if he should ever again endanger Joan's virtues.

Troopers arrive, and give chase to the Ranger. He and Tonto take cover in a barn, but a stray bullet knocks over a lamp and flames leap up around them.

CHAPTER ELEVEN: "THE SILVER BULLET"

The barn begins to collapse. Tonto and the Ranger discover a trap door and hide beneath it. Kester assumes that they have died, and decides to capture the Ranger's horse for himself. Silver and Scout refuse to be taken, and hold off Kester and his men until Tonto and the Ranger remove themselves from the wreckage of the barn. Once again, they escape from their enemies.

Jeffries, tired of Kester's failures, hires an outlaw named Morgan to capture the Lone Ranger. Bob Stewart's uncle Joe Cannon is a blacksmith and an expert gunsmith, which leads Jeffries to suspect Cannon as the source of the silver bullets. He sends Morgan and his men to investigate.

Morgan and his gang catch Cannon casting silver bullets. A tough old man, Cannon puts up quite a fight, but is shot down in cold blood. The gang rides out, taking Cannon's satchel of silver coins with them. Cannon's grandson Sammy sees them leave, and rushes into the smithy to find his grandfather's body.

Morgan and his men decide to keep the silver a secret from Jeffries, split the coins up among themselves, and toss the empty satchel aside. Bob Stewart sees this from a distance, and picks up the satchel. Sammy, seeing him with it, fires at him, shooting his hat off, but they recognize each other and exchange information. Bob swears to avenge his uncle, and gives Sammy directions to the secret cave so he can alert the other rangers.

Bob catches up with Morgan and his gang at the cantina in Pecos, and joins their poker game. One by one, the outlaws ante with large silver coins. Finally, it is Bob's turn to ante. He reaches into his pocket and slowly extends his hand across the table, hesitates a moment, and sets down two silver bullets. Morgan drops back. "The Lone Ranger!" The cantina becomes deathly quiet as everyone turns toward the table.

"You fellas better clear out," Bob tells the bystanders. "This is a private game." Everyone clears out except Bob and the killers. Bob is shot several times, but picks off every one but Morgan, who levels a shot gun at the wounded man and says, "All right, Lone Ranger, this is your finish."

CHAPTER TWELVE: "ES-CAPE"

"Oh no it isn't," says the real Lone Ranger as he steps into the room and blasts Morgan with silver bullets. The other two rangers are close behind. Troopers surround the cantina, obliging the men to climb a ladder through a trap door to the roof. In order to drop his disguise, the Lone Ranger switches gunbelts with Tonto. They manage to hold off the troopers from the rooftop, and eventually escape. Bob Stewart dies, leaving only three rangers.

Joan, meanwhile, has discovered an interesting artifact in an old desk. It is a wanted poster for one Mark Smith, who is none other than the man they know as Jeffries. She tells her father, but Jeffries/Smith discovers the poster and decides to dispose of them. He orders Kester to arrange a fatal carriage ride for the unfortunate pair. Another pigeon alerts the Lone Ranger.

The Ranger sneaks into town again, and fights a number of sentries, eventually managing to steal the carriage with Joan and her father inside. The passengers have no idea who their driver is as they are driven at breakneck speed away from Pecos with a party of troopers in hot pursuit. The chase goes on through hairpin mountain passes, as the carriage veers closer and closer to the edge of a sheer cliff.

Suddenly, the Lone Ranger loses the reins, and the coach plummets off the road.

CHAPTER THIRTEEN: "THE FATAL PLUNGE"

In the prints available, there are no credits and no recap at the start of Chapter Thirteen. In fact, this chapter and the preceding one have no break between them. The footage viewed shows the Ranger lose the reins, climb into the carriage, and jump from the careening vehicle with Joan and her father before the carriage goes over the edge. It seems likely, given the formula used in the serials, that Chapter Twelve ended with the crash as described above, and that the escape was revealed only in the opening of Chapter Thir-

teen. This may be incorrect, but it seems a reasonable guess from the information available.

Having jumped free, the Lone Ranger and the Blanchards have just enough time to conceal themselves from the troopers. Kester and his men descend to check the carriage for bodies, leaving only one man, Felton, to guard the horses. The Ranger captures him, and all four ride to the secret cave.

Tonto secures Felton with rawhide, and everyone else, including Sammy, gather around the fire. The Ranger has dropped his disguise. The Blanchards reveal their discovery of the wanted poster, and key scenes from the first episode are repeated: Smith's assumption of Jeffries' identity, the massacre of the Texas Rangers at Grant's Pass, and the climactic fight with Joe Snead at the old stockade. Once these stories are told, it is discovered that Felton has escaped his bonds.

Felton appears on an overhanging ledge, with the Lone Ranger's guns. He threatens to fire on Sammy and the Blanchards unless all the rangers come out into the open. The rangers consider shooting Felton, but Tonto warns

them that gunfire might bring down the stalactites hanging from the roof of the cave, if not the entire roof itself. Dick Forrest quietly scales the wall behind Felton, while the other two rangers step out into the open slowly. Felton becomes more and more agitated, and seems about to fire, when Forrest leaps upon him. Both men fall off the ledge.

CHAPTER FOURTEEN: "MESSENGERS OF DOOM"

Felton dies in the fall, and Forrest sustains a back injury. In Pecos, Father McKim's message pigeons are discovered. Kester releases a pigeon, rides with his men to where it was last seen, and releases another, drawing closer and closer to the secret cave. The arrival of pigeons without messages at close intervals alerts Tonto and the rangers. Burt Rogers and Allen King ride out with Tonto, leaving Forrest with the boy and the Blanchards. En route to Pecos, the Ranger dons his mask, and rescues Father McKim from his cell. Trapped by troopers, he makes a daring rooftop leap into Silver's saddle, and speeds away.

As Kester and his men reach the cave, Forrest sends his charges to a room in the back of the cave. He greets the troopers with a powder keg and a firebrand, threatening to blow them all sky-high. They fire on him, and he drops, and a few stalactites

begins to spread. More and more men leap into the saddle to join the Ranger.

Smith's men set a fire to smoke out the defenders of the cave. The Ranger is on his way back at this point. At every crossroads, riders add to his growing force of men. The tide begins to turn, and Smith is at last in retreat. Cornered by Tonto, Smith prepares to make a final stand. The Lone Ranger leaps upon him from above, and they fight, until both men roll over the edge of a precipice. Smith is finished, but so, it seems, is the Lone Ranger.

fall. Lying on his back, the wounded Forrest empties his guns at the ceiling, loosening even more stone columns. The Lone Ranger enters, guns blazing, as the entire cave seems to collapse.

The battle over, Blanchard presides over a final service in memory of the last rangers. Everyone is downcast, mourning the loss of their hero. Suddenly, they hear the cry of "Hi Yo, Silver!" The Lone Ranger rides up and assure everyone that he is alive and well. Joan asks if she can see the face behind the mask. Always a gentleman, the Ranger lifts his mask and reveals his identity to everyone: he is Allen King. The mask drops back into place, and he and his faithful Indian companion ride off together, as another cry of "Hi Yo Silver!" rings across the prairie.

CHAPTER FIFTEEN: "THE LAST OF THE RANGERS"

The Lone Ranger takes cover under an outcropping of rock as the stalactites bring death to Kester and his men. Once the dust clears, he digs Forrest out of the debris, only to witness the last breaths of yet another comrade. Another funeral is held.

Smith, his power slipping away, attacks the cave. He and his troopers are repelled and regroup. The rangers are low on ammunition, so the last two ride out to enlist aid. Silver breaks loose and follows them. One ranger is shot off his horse. The last ranger, the Lone Ranger again, dons his disguise, mounts Silver, and rides through the countryside alerting the ranchers. The word

The Lone Ranger Rides Again

The success of THE LONE RANGER in 1938 prompted Republic to immediately begin to plan a sequel. They contacted George W. Trendle on June 22, 1938, and began negotiating the rights. Talks moved along so quickly that a synopsis of the sequel (then called THE LONE RANGER RETURNS), written by Gerald Geraghty, was forwarded to Trendle on July 29, 1938. Believing that Republic would be a good studio to stick with, he even offered them the chance to film an adaptation of the then-new series, THE GREEN HORNET.

On September 2, 1938, Republic entered into an agreement with Trendle to produce their sequel to THE LONE RANGER...

This time Trendle balked at allowing them to release a feature version and the money Republic was paying Trendle more than doubled to $40,000 (instead of the previous $18,750) against 10% of the gross. This boosted the final cost of THE LONE RANGER RIDES AGAIN to $193,623 whereas the first serial (which looked more expensive overall) had cost $168,117. Actually both serials cost about the same to produce; the licensing fee being the only additional cost.

Although the Lone Ranger had been a mystery man in THE LONE RANGER, in the sequel he would be little more than a western version of Zorro as his identity would be known to the audience from the start. He'd just put on the guise of the Lone Ranger whenever he needed to go into action. George W. Trendle vigorously opposed this but Republic retained final say when it came to script control and they refused to budge on this point. This may have later led to Trendle offering Universal the rights to a third serial. Such discussions were well underway even as THE LONE RANGER RIDES AGAIN was being released. This led to the final falling out between Trendle and Republic.

Although Lee Powell had been very popular as the Lone Ranger, Republic gave Powell his walking papers when the actor demanded better scripts which made greater use of his acting abilities. Thus Republic chose to cast Bob Livingston as the lead in THE LONE RANGER RIDES AGAIN. The studio was grooming Livingston to be a major Western star alongside Roy Rogers, Gene Autry and John Wayne, but somehow he never caught on. Perhaps it bears out the old adage that stars are born, not made.

THE LONE RANGER RIDES AGAIN was not a very good serial, although it proved popular enough when released to justify interest in a third outing.

Robert Livingston was born Robert E. Randall on Dec. 9, 1908 in Quincy, Illinois. His father was an editor for the Associated Press and when Bob was twelve, the family relocated to Glendale, California. While growing up, Bob worked a number of odd jobs from ranch hand to seaman and even as a reporter for the Los Angeles Daily Times. While covering the Pasadena Community Playhouse, he became interested in acting and took classes. Following his appearance in a number of productions at the Pasadena Playhouse, he signed a contract with Universal Studios in 1929 to appear in a series of college films called the Collegiate Series. He secured other film work and was signed by MGM in 1933.

Feeling MGM was taking too long to build his career, he secured a release from his contract and went to the then-new Republic Studios. They offered him the lead in the serial THE VIGILANTES ARE COMING (which was a remake of the Rudolph Valentino silent epic THE EAGLE) in which he played a masked avenger. It was a huge success and he again donned a mask for Republic in the studio's first color production, THE BOLD CABALLERO, which was a remake of Douglas Fairbanks Sr.'s silent classic THE MARK OF ZORRO.

When Republic secured the rights to the Mesquiteer series, Bob played Stoney Brooke, one of the leads. He co-starred with Sid Saylor and Ray "Crash" Corrigan. Livingston made fifteen Mesquiteer films and it proved a highly popular series. Following THE LONE RANGER RIDES AGAIN, Livingston returned to the Mesquiteer series and made fourteen more for a total of twenty-nine of the films. Livingston left Republic in 1942 for the Producers Releasing Corporation where he made a series of films as the Lone Rider with Al "Fuzzy" St. John.

The year 1945 proved a turning point in Livingston's life and career. His brother Jack Randall, a Western star in his own right, bad-

OPPOSITE: After defeating the Black Raider and kicking him off, The Lone Ranger grabs the reins and brings the wago under control.

ly injured himself in an accident while filming the Universal serial THE ROYAL MOUNTED RIDES AGAIN, and died not long afterwards. Although some leading men seemed to age gracefully in Westerns, Livingston found himself turning to character roles. When the plans for a Lone Ranger TV series were announced in 1949, Livingston sought the role but, at 40, was passed over for the younger Clayton Moore. Livingston later appeared on the Lone Ranger in character parts with both John Hart and Clayton Moore. Livingston shortly thereafter left acting and turned to a somewhat successful second career writing screenplays. He died at the ripe old age of 83 on March 7, 1988.

In THE LONE RANGER RIDES AGAIN, even though Tonto remained the Ranger's faithful Indian companion, Duncan Re-naldo emerged to become Bill Andrews faithful Mexican companion and figured as prominently as Tonto did. Renaldo would come to be known as the Cisco Kid in the Forties in feature films and carried the role into television in a successful series in the Fifties.

Today, like the previous serial, THE LONE RANGER RIDES AGAIN exists only as an old worn print with Spanish subtitles, although the soundtrack remains in English. A rather ordinary story by serial standards, the chapter-play suffers particularly when compared to the more lavish and inventive earlier LONE RANGER. Due to the full face mask, neither serial fits comfortably today into the Lone Ranger canon as most view it.

The Lone Ranger Rides Again

DIRECTORS: William Witney
              & John English
SCREENPLAY:
          Franklyn Adreon,
Ronald Davidson, Sol Shor
        and Barry Shipman
Based on the Radio Serial "The
Lone Ranger" by Fran Striker
PRODUCTION MANAGER:
             Al Wilson
UNIT MANAGER:
         Mack D'Agostino
PHOTOGRAPHY:
   William Nobles, Edgar Lyons
FILM EDITORS: Helene Turner,
            Edward Todd
MUSICAL DIRECTOR:
         Alberto Colombo

CAST
BILL ANDREWS:
        Robert Livingston
THE LONE RANGER:
        Robert Livingston
THE LONE RANGER'S VOICE:
        Bill Bletcher
TONTO: Chief Thunder Cloud
SILVER: Silver Chief
JUAN VASQUEZ:
        Duncan Renaldo
SUE DOLAN: Jinx Falken
BART DOLAN: Ralph Dunn
CRAIG DOLAN:
        J. Farrell MacDonald
JED SCOTT: William Gould
EVANS: Rex Lease
MERRITT: Ted Mapes
PA DANIELS: Henry Otho
MA DANIELS: Betty Roadman
HARDIN: John Beach
THORNE: Glenn Strange
MURDOCK: Stanley Blystone
HANK: Eddie Parker

COLT: Al Taylor
LOGAN: Carleton Young
BLACK: Charles Whitaker
BLACKIE: Rob Robinson
BILL: Ralph LeFever
HEAVY ONE: Charles Regan
HEAVY TWO: Fred Schaefer
HEAVY THREE: David Sharpe
HEAVY FOUR: Art Felix
HEAVY FIVE: Chick Hannon
COOPER: Eddie Dean
DANNY DANIELS:
        Bob McClung
DEPUTY: Duke Lee
MARTIN GIBSON:
        Howard Chase
GROVER: Ernie Adams
JOHNNY: Nelson McDowell
JONES: Walter Wills
SAM LAWSON: Jack Kirk
LONG: Fred Burns
LUKE: Buddy Mason
LYNCH: Lew Meehan
MANNY: Wheeler Oakman
MILLER: Forrest Taylor
JOE PARKER: Frank Ellis
POSSEMAN ONE: Herman Hack
POSSEMAN TWO: Bill Yrigoyen
POSSEMAN THREE:
        Wesley Hopper
POSSEMAN FOUR: Bud Wolfe
POSSEMAN FIVE:
        Joe Yriggoyen
POSSEMAN SIX: Duke Taylor
POSSEMAN SEVEN:
        Forest Burns
POSSEMAN EIGHT:
        George DeNormand
ED POWERS: George Burton
STRIKER: Tommy Coats
HOLMES: Howard Hickey
GEORGE: Barry Hays
CASS: Ted Wells
REX: Burt Dillard
MACK: Cecil Kellogg
GILL: Carl Sepulveda
RANCE: Buddy Messenger
SAFE HEAVY: Jerome Ward
SHERIFF: Roger Williams
SLADE: Buddy Roosevelt
SMITH: Jack Montgomery

STAGE DRIVER: Post Parks
STAGE GUARD: Art Dillard
TOWNSMAN ONE: Horace Carpenter
TOWNSMAN TWO:
　　　　　Cactus Mack
TOWNSMAN THREE:
　　　　　Lafe McKee
TOWNSMAN FOUR:
　　　　　Augie Gomez
TOWNSMAN FIVE:
　　　　　Charles Hutchison
TUCKER: Monte Montague
E.B. TULLY: Griff Barnette
DIEGO VASQUEZ: Joe Perez

CHAPTER ONE: "THE LONE RANGER RETURNS"

The setting is New Mexico, during the period when newly arriving homesteaders began moving into regions originally claimed by the cattlemen. The story opens with the burning of the Vasquez family ranchero. Juan Vasquez arrives upon this scene in time to witness the death of his brother, Diego, who has been shot in the back. Before he expires, Diego claims to have been shot by the Lone Ranger. Juan is determined to take revenge.

In his pursuit of the Ranger, Juan encounters a group of homesteaders, the Daniels family, who share water with him (somewhat grudgingly) and tell him that he is only a few hours behind his prey. Soon enough, he catches up with the masked man and confronts him at gunpoint.

"You might be making a mistake," cautions the Ranger, but Vasquez is certain he is right. The Ranger tricks him into thinking that Tonto has the drop on him, and knocks him off his horse. They fight until the Ranger gets the upper hand. He asks Juan to give him three days to clear himself, and will not relent until Juan gives him his word. He then returns Juan's guns as a gesture of trust.

They ride toward San Ramon, New Mexico. Tonto joins them along the way. As they ride, the Ranger talks of upcoming trouble between the ranchers and the homesteaders. Jed Scott, the leader of the homesteaders, is due to arrive in New Mexico very soon.

On the morning of the third day, Juan wakes up to find his escorts gone. He heads in toward San Ramon alone. At the same time, the Jed Scott party has been seen approaching by a group of armed men, who plan to attack the homesteaders when they reach Torry Pass. Juan, riding in from another direction, sees the ambush being prepared and warns Jed Scott and the wagon train he's leading. A gun battle follows and soon, with the help of Juan, the attackers are

49

another room, only to be shot from the window. Scott draws his gun and prepares to pursue the shooter, but when others burst into the room they accuse Scott of Grover's murder and arrest him. As Jed Scott is led away, one of the men in the room slips out the window. When he is seen again, it is in the familiar garb of the Lone Ranger. He intercepts Scott, frees him, and they ride out of town.

When the alarm is raised, Juan is the first one to pursue the Ranger. Andrews is close behind. When the Ranger and Scott split up, Juan stays on the Ranger's trail while Andrews goes after Scott. Juan soon corners the Lone Ranger and guns him down!

Andrews arrives on the scene and he and Juan unmask the Lone Ranger. He's revealed to be Logan, a local man who says that Grover was actually shot by a man named Slade. Juan expresses amazement that Logan could be the Lone Ranger. Andrews suggests that Logan is an impostor and reveals his own identity by repeating, in a deeper voice, words he had spoken to Juan in the heat of their fight three days earlier. Juan has been riding with the Lone Ranger without even realizing it. They become friends. Logan dies, paying for the death of Diego Vas-

repelled. The homesteaders capture a wounded man and someone recognizes him as a man who works for Craig Dolan, the cattleman, and a sworn opponent of the homesteaders. They take the man to San Ramon and confront Dolan. He disavows any connection with the man, having fired him the week before. He also expresses his opposition to the homesteaders. The main problem between the ranchers and the settlers seems to concern water rights. Scott and Dolan agree to meet later, to discuss the water rights issue.

That night, at the Oasis Hotel and Cantina, Scott waits for Dolan. Juan and another man, Andrews (who had joined the Scott party on the way and taken their side in the gun battle) are there as well. "Doc" Grover approaches Scott with important news about the water rights and takes him into quez. The Ranger then sends Scott back to the sheriff while he investigates the murder of Doc Grover.

Meanwhile, Dolan's men make plans to incite the settlers into freeing Scott from jail. By convincing them that Scott may be killed while in jail, they hope to bring them into town where they can wipe out many of the homesteaders while "helping" the sheriff defend the jail.

The Ranger finds Slade's hideout and learns a remarkable fact. Grover is not really dead, his murder having been faked with blanks in the gun. The Ranger breaks in and fights Slade and his men while Grover cowers in a corner. In due time, the Ranger gains control of the situation. A rider brings news of the plan to incite the settlers; the Ranger listens, covering Slade and his men from behind the door.

The settlers, by now, have reached the jail. The situation grows tense, but Juan talks them into returning to their camp. One of Dolan's men shoots out a window before they can leave, and starts a gunfight. As the battle rages, a stray bullet breaks a lamp and starts a fire in the jailhouse. The sheriff and his deputy try to rescue Scott, but the flames keep them away from the cell door. The Ranger arrives and rushes in to save the innocent man, draping a blanket over his head and braving the flames. But as he enters the jail cell, the roof caves in.

CHAPTER TWO: "MASKED VICTORY"

Juan brings Silver to the jailhouse wall, ties a rope to the bars in the window and pulls out a section of the wall. The Lone Ranger

and Jed Scott escape just seconds before the roof caves in.

The next day, Scott stands trial for the murder of Doc Grover. He enters a plea of not guilty. When the Lone Ranger speaks, Dolan protests the presence of a masked man in court. Judge Miller will hear none of this. "The Lone Ranger has the respect of all law-abiding people," he tells Dolan. "He stands for justice."

The Ranger then reveals that Grover is still alive. The court recesses for half an hour in order to give Tonto time to bring Grove and Slade to town. But on the way, Tonto is captured by Dolan's men and is taken, with his charges, to a secret cave hideout.

The court recess ends with no sign of Tonto. The trial must proceed. The Ranger brings up the question of Grover's body. A murder cannot be proven if there is no corpse. Judge Miller agrees, and so the entire courtroom packs up and heads out to Grover's ranch, the alleged site of his grave.

The Ranger searches for Tonto and finds Scout.

Some of Dolan's men are already at the ranch and are digging a grave to put Grover in, a simple enough solution to their problem. In the cave, Grover is about to die after all, only to be finally saved by the Lone Ranger. A fight follows; Grover unties Tonto and the tide turns in the Ranger's favor.

Meanwhile, everyone else has reached the ranch to find the fresh, empty grave. Dolan attempts to incite a lynching of Scott. His men throw a rope over a tree and are about to hang Jed when the Ranger arrives with Grover. When the Ranger singles out Slade as the man behind the frame-up of Scott, Slade draws his gun and shoots the Ranger off his horse.

CHAPTER THREE: "THE BLACK RAIDERS STRIKE"

The Lone Ranger accuses Slade of the plot against Jed Scott. Slade pulls his gun and shoots the Ranger, who falls from his saddle to the ground. Juan shoots Slade. The Ranger gets up, having only been bruised. His sack of silver (from which he molds bullets) had stopped the bullet and saved his life. Slade is not so lucky.

Scott plans a meeting at the Land Office the next day. He tells Bart, Dolan's nephew, to tell Dolan to be there.

At the meeting, Scott reveals to Dolan that an act of Congress has opened up the water rights in New Mexico to the homesteaders. Dolan gives in but tells the settlers that their task won't be easy, especially with the vigilante Black Raiders around. The ranchers won't be able to help against them, he says.

The Lone Ranger and his two sidekicks follow Bart Dolan as he heads into the badlands to meet the Black Raiders. Bart tells the Raiders to attack the Daniels family at Willow Springs.

After this exchange, the Ranger follows the Raiders while Juan and Tonto track Bart. Bart's horse has a broken shoe, making the tracking easy. But Bart meets his sister, Sue, who is heading back to town, and trades horses with her. Tonto loses the trail.

The Ranger draws close to the Raider camp, but is attacked from behind. He escapes but is pursued. Sue enters the scene and helps him escape. The Black Raiders decide to let him go for now and head for the Daniels encampment. The Ranger sends Sue into town to tell Jed Scott of the danger to the Daniels family.

The Ranger reaches Willow Springs just in time to help the Daniels family defend their position against the Raiders. Their ammunition begins to run low, though.

Sue reaches town and alerts Scott, but Juan sees the broken shoe on her horse and decides that her story is a trick. They will not go to Willow Springs.

The Ranger talks the Daniels family into abandoning their camp and goods to save their lives. He covers them, then makes his own escape before the smoke clears. The settlers have avoided crossing the river because of heavy mud on its floor, but the Ranger doesn't realize this. As he crosses the river on foot, he begins sinking into the mud which slowly pulls him beneath the surface of the water.

CHAPTER FOUR: "THE CAVERN OF DOOM"

Tonto arrives, throws the Ranger a rope and pulls him free. The Raiders have stolen the wagon containing the Daniels' provisions, so they try to get it back. The Raider driving the wagon is knocked off, and the Lone Ranger takes the reins.

Sue, suspicious of her brother, follows him. Bart knows she is tailing him so he plans to have some Raiders attack him and tie him up in order to fool her. She falls for it easily enough, but manages to find the Lone Ranger. He and Tonto join her to rescue Bart. They trail the Raiders to another secret cave hideaway. Joan falls back while the two men go in. They get the drop on the Raiders but Bart, his hands tied, manages to pull a bullet from his belt and toss it into the fire. The explosion distracts the good guys, and another fistfight takes place. Two Raiders and Bart make their way to the door of the cave and trap the Ranger and Tonto by locking a large gate across the inner opening of the cave. They then set a powderkeg alight to kill the Ranger and close the opening of their now useless hideout. Trapped, the heroes struggle with the lock, then attempt to put out the fuse with a long stick. The episode ends with the sound of an explosion over the credits.

CHAPTER FIVE: "AGENTS OF DECEIT"

The Lone Ranger and Tonto whistle for their horses. The Ranger calls to Silver. The horse rides in and and the Ranger coaxes Silver into rolling the powderkeg out of the cave, where it explodes without injuring anyone. Not far off, Bart and the Black Raiders hear the explosion and think they have killed the Ranger. Silver and Scout pull down the gate so that the Ranger and Tonto can escape.

Sue runs into the party of Raiders, who have Bart tied up. The Lone Ranger comes across this group. In the ensuing fight, Sue's horse bolts and the Ranger races to save her. He succeeds, then escorts her and Bart back to town. There he asks Dolan to try to get along with Scott and the homesteaders.

Alone with Bart, Dolan tells him that he still plans to fight the homesteaders, but only through legal means.

The homesteaders receive a wagon of seed, which is vital to their survival. The next day, Scott and his men have a meeting with Dolan and leave three men to guard the seed. While the meeting is go-

ing on, Bart sends men to destroy the seed.

Bill Andrews slips out of the meeting, dons his mask and he and Tonto ride to the settlers' camp. They arrive to find a burning wagon, rolled downhill by the Black Raiders, barrelling right towards the seed wagon. The Ranger jumps right onto the careening wagon.

CHAPTER SIX: "THE TRAP"

The Ranger diverts the course of the burning wagon and jumps free. Tonto, Scott and the homesteaders return and drive off the Raiders.

A stagecoach is on its way to San Ramon, bearing the official government land claim forms. The Black Raiders rob the coach. Tonto tracks them. He and the Lone Ranger find the Raiders trying to break open the strongbox. The Ranger leads the Raiders on a chase, and when the Raiders return they find the box empty, except for four silver bullets. The homesteaders receive the forms and make their claims.

The Land Office clerk stores the

CHAPTER SEVEN: "THE LONE RANGER AT BAY"

Two Black Raiders arrive just as the Lone Ranger dials the last number. They make him step aside and one of the Raiders receives the fatal blast of buckshot. The Rang-

claim forms in the jail safe. The sheriff rigs a gun to the safe door, so that anyone opening the safe will be shot.

Two of Bart's men, Rance and Blackie, plan to kidnap the clerk and torture the combination out of him. Tonto overhears these plans. That night, the Ranger, Tonto and Juan go to the barn where the clerk has been taken. The clerk gives up the combination to avoid being beaten, and the Ranger overhears, leaps on his horse and heads into town to get the claims first.

Juan and Tonto break into the barn and rescue the clerk. He tells them of the boobytrap on the safe. They follow the Ranger, but he is already turning the dial of the safe. The episode ends with the sound of a gunshot over the credits.

er knocks out the other Raider and makes off with the claims.

In the morning, Dolan demands that the sheriff get the claims back so the clerk can examine them before they are sent to Washington. Dolan does not want to take the chance that the settlers might alter the claims before sending them in. Dolan sends some of his men with the sheriff, and Bart offers them a $5000 reward for killing the Ranger.

The sheriff and his posse reach Scott's headquarters just as he is hiding the papers. Andrews and Juan stage a fight to distract the sheriff, giving Scott time to conceal the documents. The sheriff cannot find them. He rides off, but only out of sight so he can watch for any riders from Scott's camp.

Andrews follows the sheriff and warns the settlers that they're be ing watched. He comes up with a plan.

Juan and Andrews ride out clutching sheaves of paper in their hands while another man prepares to carry the real documents. The sheriff and his posse chase them. Juan and Andrews meet Tonto; Andrews becomes the Lone Ranger once more and rides toward the posse with the papers in his hand. The posse corners him in a shack at the base of a tall rock formation. They send two men to climb down around the back, but they set off a landslide directly above the shack.

CHAPTER EIGHT: "AMBUSH"

As the rocks begin to fall, the Lone Ranger whistles for Silver. They escape seconds before the landslide crushes the cabin and kills the sheriff.

It becomes necessary to elect a new sheriff. The settlers nominate Pa Daniels as their candidate, while the ranchers put forward deputy Joe Parker as theirs.

Black Raiders kidnap Danny Daniels to dissuade his father from running. Pa Daniels goes to Painted Gorge to save Danny when he learns of the news. Sue, at the Daniels house, leaves to get help. Pa Daniels shoots one of the Raider sentries. They ride away. Daniels goes into the cave and gets the drop on four Raiders, only to be captured from behind by a fifth.

Sue meets with the Lone Ranger and explains the situation. He rides to the cave and interrupts one of the Raiders who's slapping Pa Daniels. He gives the two Daniels men his guns and teaches the Raider a lesson with his fists. Then they tie up all five Raiders and head out of the cave. The un-wounded sentry has returned and is waiting outside to shoot the first man out of the cave.

CHAPTER NINE: "WHEELS OF DOOM"

The Raider fires, winging Pa Daniels. Not being in Raider uniform, he and his companion claim to have been tracking the Raiders themselves, and that the shooting of Daniels was a mistake.

Bart watches as the Ranger makes the men assemble a stretcher for Daniels and carry him away. Bart then sneaks into the cave to untie the five Raiders.

Daniels will live but will be an invalid for awhile. He suggests Jed Scott as his replacement. The settlers arrange a write-in campaign. While the Ranger goes to fetch Scott from a distant camp, the doctor informs Bart of this news.

The Raiders ambush Scott, Tonto and the Ranger, but the men see them in time to take cover. As their ammo runs low, the Ranger plans to hold off the Raiders alone. Then he and Tonto come up with a better plan. Tonto falls as if shot, fooling the Raiders. Scott and the Ranger make a run for it. The Raiders pursue them only to be caught in a crossfire as Tonto rides out behind them. The Raiders retreat.

That evening the balloting is finished and the ballots are to be stored overnight. The settlers outnumber the ranchers two to one, so they expect foul play, and set up guards in town. Bart arranges for the ballots to be stolen. One of his men fakes drunkenness and weaves up and down the street trying to light his pipe. Before this he has put pepper in the bowl of the pipe. When a guard helps him out with a light, he blows pepper into the man's face, knocks him out, steals the ballots and tosses them into a passing covered wagon. Bart's plan is to erase the write-in votes and change them so his candidate wins.

The Lone Ranger chases the wagon, leaps into it and fights a man in the back of it. The bad guy's gun goes off, shooting the driver while the fight goes on. The strongbox with the ballots in it fall out of the wagon, which runs out of control down a very steep hill.

CHAPTER TEN: "THE DANGEROUS CAPTIVE"

The Ranger leaps to safety before the wagon crashes. He whistles for Silver and takes the ballots back to town.

Scott is elected sheriff. He appoints four men as his deputies: Evans, Powers, Juan Vasquez and Andrews. Bart plots to keep the deputies busy by having some Raiders, led by a man named Lynch, "rustle" some of his uncle's cattle. Dolan asks the new sheriff for help. The deputies investigate, but Juan and Andrews find it interesting that there should be such an upswing in rustling just after the election.

Tonto and the Ranger find the cattle and see an ambush being set up for the deputies. Tonto goes to warn the deputies but is pursued and lassoed by two Raiders. The other three deputies almost ride into the ambush. A gunfight ensues until the Ranger appears behind the Raiders and saves the day. Tonto is freed. The Ranger captures Lynch and takes him in to Sheriff Scott.

The Raiders plan to keep Lynch from talking by blowing up the jail. They set powderkegs behind the jail and take up positions behind a wall of sandbags. Alerted, Andrews and Juan exchange fire with the Raiders. Juan is shot in the shoulder. Andrews makes his way up to the roof of the jail as the fuse grows shorter.

CHAPTER ELEVEN" DEATH BELOW"

Andrews lassoes the burning powderkeg from the roof and swings it over to the sandbag barrier, where it blows up in the Raiders' faces. Juan turns out to have been nicked, but nothing more.

It is learned that Gibson, the Federal Land Registrar, is on the way to San Ramon. He has the authority to arbitrate in all land matters, and the power to call in the cavalry to enforce his decisions. Dolan is not too happy about this news. Still, the Ranger is not convinced that Dolan is behind the Black Raiders. He thinks it could be someone else but does not know who.

Bart sends men to bribe Gibson, if possible. They attack his stagecoach, killing the driver and guard, but Gibson refuses to be bought. The Raiders take him to their hideout after an attack by the Ranger.

The Ranger and Tonto capture a wounded Raider and he leads them to the hideout. He breaks open the door and fights the two Raiders guarding Gibson as more Raiders approach on horseback. Gibson frees himself and helps the Ranger with a well-aimed chair to the head of a Raider. The mounted Raiders are almost there, so Gibson and the Ranger go out the back door. Tonto scales a high rock outcropping behind the hideout and lowers a rope. Gibson climbs up as the rope begins to fray.

The Ranger takes his turn but the rope breaks and he falls.

CHAPTER TWELVE: "BLAZING PERIL"

The Lone Ranger lands in some bushes. He throws the broken rope up to Tonto, who ties it back together, enabling the Ranger to escape.

Scott and Gibson meet. Gibson declares his intent to investigate both sides of the dispute. He will hear the settlers' side that night, at Freeman's barn. When Dolan learns of the meeting he is very angry.

At the meeting, events of earlier chapters are reviewed. Gibson learns of the attempt to frame Jed Scott with the phony murder, as well as about the false Lone Ranger.

Meanwhile, Black Raiders sneak up on Freeman's barn. They set it on fire, trapping everyone, including Andrews, inside.

CHAPTER THIRTEEN: "EXPOSED"

Everyone trapped in the barn goes into the grain cellar through a trap door and wait out the fire in safety. The Raiders, certain that they have wiped out everyone, ride away. Gibson plans to confront Dolan. But the Lone Ranger, as Andrews, is not entirely certain that Dolan is the man behind the Black Raiders.

They ride back into town. A Raider sees them and rushes to inform Bart. Dolan overhears them

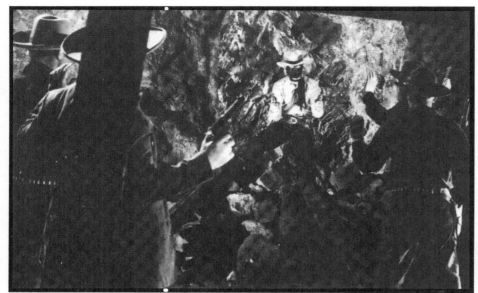

his men. The Ranger gets behind the Raiders and gets the drop on them, only to trip and stumble. Bart is about to shoot the Ranger when Tonto shoots the gun out of Bart's hand. Bart and Tonto fight. A posse arrives. Bart and his men flee into the depths of the mine through a narrow tunnel with a track for mining carts. The Ranger follows. Bart rolls an old mining cart down the incline towards the Ranger, whose only hope is to outrun the cart.

and learns that Bart is behind the Black Raiders. He becomes angry. "Dolans have always been fighters," he tells Bart. "You're the first one that hasn't fought square." He plans to turn Bart over to the sheriff. Bart shoots him. Then, hearing Sue approach, he shoots two holes in the window. Sue enters the room through one door, Juan through another. Bart claims that the Lone Ranger shot Dolan through the window.

The Ranger and Tonto arrive. The Ranger points out that the holes in the window screen are punched outwards, proving that the shots came from inside. Bart holds his own sister at gunpoint and makes the men drop their guns. He then herds them and Sue into a small room and locks them there.

While Bart rides off, the Ranger breaks open the door. Dolan is seriously wounded, but not fatally so. Dolan tells the Ranger of Bart's connection to the Black Raiders.

Bart joins the Black Raiders at their hideout, an abandoned mine. He plans to attack the settlers. The Lone Ranger and Tonto trail him to the hideout, knock out the sentry and exchange fire with Bart and

CHAPTER FOURTEEN: "BE-SIEGED"

The Lone Ranger blocks the track with a piece of wood, successfully derailing the cart. He and Tonto head back to Dolan's ranch. Dolan is wounded but will live. He warns that Bart will be crazy for revenge now that his plans have been thwarted. Bart wants to wage out and out war on the settlers. The remaining Black Raiders are dubious about the risk of facing Federal cavalry, but Bart is obsessed with going on. He vows to round up every rustler and outlaw in the territory to fight for him.

Once this force is raised it first attacks the Evans homestead. Andrews and the deputies, including Evans, see smoke from the raid. They arrive there just as the Raiders are leaving and Andrews lassoes one. The captured man tells them of Bart's army. They send out an alert for the settlers to occupy the old fort.

The settlers head for the fort, all the while being harassed by Bart's marauders. Juan warns one family and helps them escape from pursuit. The Ranger helps a wagon reach the fort, all the while under fire. The area around the fort is already a battle zone. Bart's men mass outside just as the last of the settlers reaches the precarious safety of the fort. The Ranger, as Andrews, rides out to draw them away from the fort, only to encounter another group of them. The episode ends as he is chased across the countryside.

CHAPTER FIFTEEN: "FRONTIER JUSTICE"

The chase goes on. A shot rings out and Andrews falls from his horse. His pursuers leave him for dead. It's only a trick, though, and when they're gone Andrews whistles for Silver and dons his mask. Once again Raiders pursue him, but he eludes them and rides at breakneck speed to get help.

Bart and his men launch a wave of attacks on the fort designed to draw the settlers' fire and waste their limited supply of ammunition. Bart watches from the hill as his men do all the fighting. After several attacks he sends some men to get the powder wagon from a nearby quarry.

The Lone Ranger reaches the cavalry post and alerts them to the situation. The cavalry rides out behind him.

The Raiders charge the fort again. The settlers are almost out of ammunition. When the powder wagon arrives, Bart has the horses unhitched, a powderkeg lit, and rolls the wagon down towards the gate of the fort. The settlers run away from the gate.

The Ranger arrives ahead of the cavalry and jumps aboard the wagon. The wagon stops right at the gate. The Ranger holds off the Raiders and they retreat, then goes inside the wagon. He then scales the fence and tells the settlers to clear away from the gate.

Bart thinks that the Ranger has doused the fuse and rides down to relight it. As Bart climbs into the wagon, he discovers that the Ranger has left the fuse burning! All he can manage is a brief look of dismay as he and the wagon blow sky-high.

The Raiders attack the now-demolished gate. All seems lost but then the cavalry arrives and encircles the Raiders. The battle is over.

Dolan and Scott swear to live in peace. They ask the Lone Ranger to stay, but he and Tonto must ride wherever justice and oppression exist. He declines to reveal his face to anyone. He says goodbye to his friend Juan Vasquez, and then he and Tonto are off, with a final cry of "Hi-Yo Silver!"

Good luck always
The Lone Ranger
& TONTO

The Lone Ranger On Television

Although it's not known why, owner George W. Trendle did not market serial or feature rights to the Lone Ranger after Universal Studios dropped their interest in the property in 1939. In light of Universal producing two Green Hornet serials in 1940 from another property owned by Trendle, this is quite surprising. Westerns were very popular in the Thirties and Forties and continued as a staple for many studios due to how inexpensive they were to produce. Roy Rogers, Gene Autry, Buster Crabbe, the Durango Kid, the Cisco Kid and others appeared regularly throughout the Forties, but not the Lone Ranger. Not until television came into its own did Trendle link up with Hollywood once more.

A pioneer in the theater chain business in the Twenties, and in radio in the Thirties, Trendle saw this new entertainment medium as possessing unlimited possibilities, and being the wave of the future. Another believer in the future of the medium, Western star William Boyd went into debt to buy up

Merita Bread was the original sponsor of the Lone Ranger television series.

all rights to his Hopalong Cassidy motion pictures and became a multi-millionaire in the Fifties from licensing the broadcast rights to product-hungry television stations.

General Mills, a long-time sponsor of the Lone Ranger radio series, was first to be offered the opportunity to become involved in this burgeoning medium called television with the Lone Ranger. Trendle said that if they sponsored the TV show, it would be under the same terms as the radio show, General Mills would pay all production costs while Trendle's company The Lone Ranger, Inc. would oversee production. General Mills would exercise no creative control. Trendle disliked the fights he'd had with Republic when they made unnecessary changes in the Lone Ranger in their serials and wanted to insure this celluloid version of the

masked rider of the plains would be absolutely faithful to what listeners heard three times a week on radio.

Someone recommended Jack Chertock to Trendle and he went with this producer and his Apex Film Corporation to produce the Lone Ranger for television. Apparently Chertock and Trendle had a lot in common as both were tight with the dollar. "He was probably one of the cheapest guys that ever worked in Hollywood," said John Hart in describing Jack Chertock. Hart played the Lone Ranger after Clayton Moore quit in a pay dispute, and Hart said he was glad when his stint was over due to how little he was paid.

George Seitz was hired as one of the directors and screenwriters of the series. He worked with Fran Striker to adapt the radio series faithfully to television. The first three episodes of the TV series formed an expanded origin adapted from radio scripts. A number of actors tried out for the part of the Lone Ranger, including Robert Livingston who had played the lead in the serial THE LONE RANGER RIDES AGAIN in 1939, and Brace Beemer, who continued to do the voice of the Lone Ranger on radio. Clayton Moore won the role, with Jay Silverheels as Tonto.

Clayton Moore was born in Chicago on September 14, 1914. In his youth he worked in the circus as a trapeze artist, and when he got into films in 1939, he worked as a stunt man as well as an actor. In 1942 he co-starred in PERILS OF NYOKA and then served in the Air Force from 1943 to 1945. Upon his release Moore continued his film work, appearing as both heavies and heroes in such serials as THE CRIMSON GHOST

(1946), JESSE JAMES RIDES AGAIN (1947), G-MEN NEVER FORGET (1947), THE ADVENTURES OF FRANK AND JESSE JAMES (1948) and GHOST OF ZORRO (1949). Moore appeared in the latter right before being cast as the Lone Ranger, which some have noted is ironic as Zorro was one of Trendle's influences behind the masked rider of the plains. When Moore quit playing the Lone Ranger for a few years over a pay dispute, he starred in such films as SON OF GERONIMO, BUFFALO BILL IN TOMAHAWK TERRITORY as well as the serials RADAR MEN FROM THE MOON (1952), JUNGLE DRUMS OF AFRICA (1952) and GUNFIGHTERS OF THE NORTHWEST (1953). Moore returned to the role in 1954 after Trendle decided to give Moore his raise rather than casting a third actor in the part. Moore remained in the role through the end of the series in 1957 and starred in two features, one in 1956 and another in 1958.

Jay Silverheels, born Harold J. Smith in Ontario, Canada on the Six Nations Indian Reservation in 1918, got the name Silverheels from a tribal elder. Under his given name of Harold J. Smith he emigrated to the United States in 1935. Although he wanted to use his Indian name, the Canadian government insisted he use his birth name. He changed his name legally to Jay Silverheels some years later.

After arriving in the US, Jay entered the Golden Gloves Tournament and finished second in the finals held at Madison Square Garden. In 1937, while playing on a professional lacrosse team in Hollywood, he was noticed by co-median Joe E. Brown who encouraged him to try his hand at acting. Jay succeeded in landing bit parts in small films, mostly Westerns, but in 1947 took a supporting role in the Tyrone Power film CAPTAIN FROM CASTILE as an Aztec warrior. His other feature film appearances include THE PRAIRIE (1947), KEY LARGO (1948), FURY AT FURNACE CREEK (1948), BROKEN ARROW (1950), RED MOUNTAIN (1951), BRAVE WARRIOR (1952), WAR ARROW (1953), THE LONE RANGER (1956), WALK THE PROUD LAND (1956), THE LONE RANGER AND THE LOST CITY OF GOLD (1958), INDIAN PAINT (1965), THE SPHYNX (1970), THE MAN WHO LOVED CAT DANCING (1973) SANTEE (1973) and TRUE GRIT (1978). Jay usually played honorable Indians in roles that did not demean his heritage. He appeared in nearly all 221 episodes of THE LONE RANGER except those he missed when he suffered a heart attack in 1954 (when he was only 36). So as not to disrupt the series more than necessary, since Tonto was written into every script, production was suspended for a few weeks. When they resumed, Jay wound up missing only four episodes. These four episodes were spread out in the continuity when aired so that his absence would not be noticed. Committed to helping Indians in Hollywood, Silverheels founded the Indian Actors Workshop in the late 1960s. In 1973 he suffered a debilitating stroke. In the summer of 1979 he received a star on the Hollywood Walk of Fame to honor him for his years of honorable portrayals of Indians on the silver screen, just one year before, on March 5, 1980, he died at the age of 62 at the Motion Picture Country Home and Hospital. Moore wept openly at Jay's funeral and stated, "I thought of him as a brother. I loved him very much and I'll miss him. He was my kemo sabe, which we all know means faithful friend. Jay was a fighter for the Indian people. The Indian cause was utmost in his mind at all times."

As mentioned earlier, the first three episodes unfolded the origin of the Lone Ranger, his special bond with Tonto, his acquisition of the great stallion Silver and the capture of the Butch Cavendish gang. Tonto and young John Reid had first met as boys when Reid saved Tonto's life. The name "kemo sabe" meant variously "faithful friend" or "trusty scout." Usually it held the former meaning on the radio show and the latter on TV. For a short period the Ranger and Tonto rode double on Scout until their chance encounter with Silver. The name of the Ranger's arch-enemy, Butch Cavendish, was inspired by the infamous real-life outlaw Butch Cassidy. Incidentally, these first three episodes are the only ones in which the Lone Ranger wears his standard-issue Texas Ranger gunbelt with only one holster. In the fourth episode he has switched without comment or explanation to the double-holster belt he would wear for the remainder of the series and two theatrical films. Tonto always wears a featherband with no feather in it, again with no explanation. These three episodes are the sole multi-part program in the series. They were later edited into one continuous story titled "The Legend Of The Lone Ranger" (not to be confused with the later 1981 film of the same title) which ran 54 minutes, pared down

from the three episodes' original 77 minutes and apparently first telecast by ABC-TV in this form in 1956.

Unlike television today where TV seasons are shot season by season, in the early Fifties different companies had their own ways of shooting shows. The first 78 episodes were shot in 1949 and 1950 and aired back-to-back from September of 1949 through March of 1951. When Moore quit, no new episodes were shot until John Hart was hired in 1952 to star in 52 episodes of THE LONE RANGER also shot back-to-back. Those episodes then aired in series and were rerun the following year. Although TV GUIDE began publishing in 1953, consulting this and other sources confirms that this is how the show was scheduled. The concept of a new show having a year and a half of reruns before new episodes aired is as unheard of today as having 52 weeks of new shows with no reruns, but such was the experimental nature of scheduling in the early years of television. A solid year of reruns was not considered that radical a notion then since such a small percentage of the American audience owned TV sets in those days.

There were a number of notable guest stars throughout the 221 episode run of THE LONE RANGER. One story going around has DeForest Kelley (STAR TREK'S Dr. McCoy) as a member of the Butch Cavendish gang in the origin story. This isn't true and is no doubt a slip of someone's memory as Kelley actually appeared in the fourth episode, the first of the regular series following the origin trilogy. Kelley also appeared in episode #117 when his friend John Hart was playing the Lone Ranger. Bob Livingston, who had tried un-

successfully to land the part of the masked man in 1949, actually guest-starred on some of the series episodes, including #85 and #133. Lane Chandler may not be a familiar name, but in the 1938 Republic serial THE LONE RANGER he was one of the five suspected of being the masked man. He turned up in a number of the TV episodes, including #8, #20 and #50. The voice of the Lone Ranger in both Republic serials was Billy Bletcher, a diminutive actor whose height belied his powerful bass voice. He appeared in episode #27. James Arness, who'd go on to star in the long-running Western series GUNSMOKE, guest-starred in episode #33 of THE LONE RANGER. John Hart, who would portray the masked rider of the planes in episodes #78 through 130, first caught the eye of the series producers when he guest-starred in episodes #34 and #46. Tom Tyler, a Western star in the Thirties and Forties, and who played the title role in the Republic serial THE ADVENTURES OF CAPTAIN MARVEL (1940), appeared in episode #39. Craig Stevens, who would go on to star in the PETER GUNN series, guest-starred in episode #35. Guy Williams, who would star in both ZORRO and LOST IN SPACE on television, appeared in episode #172. The guest star who would go on to achieve the greatest recognition was Lee Van Cleef. Then a young and struggling unknown, he appeared in episodes #82, #114 and #124, all during the tenure of the John Hart Lone Ranger.

On August 3, 1954, it was announced that George W. Trendle had sold the rights to the Lone Ranger to the Jack Wrather Corporation for a reported three mil-

lion dollars. Trendle said later that he chose to sell out then because he was getting on in years and was afraid that if he died while still owning the property it would be tied up in probate court for years while the estate tried to set a value on it. Trendle already had episodes of the Lone Ranger in production which began airing in September of 1954. As the new owner of the property, Wrather chose to increase the production values of the series. Many of the black and white episodes suffer from overuse of what they called the "green set," which was a soundstage made up to look like an exterior location, but which even a child could recognize as an indoor set due to the change in lighting and sound qualities. Many old TV series, including the Sixties hit BONANZA, suffer from this when viewed today. On THE LONE RANGER, characters would ride around a rock or bring their steeds to a halt and when they dismounted they'd suddenly be on the obviously indoor set meant to be the outside of someone's house or even just a rocky campsite. Wrather's company returned to the standard set in the earliest episodes where a great deal of location shooting was done. These last 39 episodes in the series, which were shot by Wrather's production company, were filmed in color. That the future of television would be in color productions was already foreseen in the mid-Fifties as other shows, such as THE ADVENTURES OF SUPERMAN and THE CISCO KID, shot a number of their later episodes in color. Although three million dollars was considered a high price for the Lone Ranger property in those days, Wrather quickly recouped his investment by producing two motion pictures, THE LONE RANGER (1956) and THE LONE RANGER AND THE LOST CITY OF GOLD (1958). The second film was produced after the TV series itself had gone out of first-run production and was in reruns on the networks.

Following the cancellation of the series, Clayton Moore continued to make appearances as the Lone Ranger, complete with mask. He took this very seriously and wouldn't pose for photographs without the mask, saying it would violate his contract with the Jack Wrather Corporation which didn't allow him to appear as the Lone Ranger without his mask. This contract elapsed when Moore stopped playing the Lone Ranger on screen. Unlike Adam West and Burt Ward, who paid Warner Communications a licensing fee to appear in public as Batman and Robin, Clayton Moore had no such arrangement. This led to problems later when Warner Brothers was producing a new LONE RANGER film in 1981 and the Wrather Corp. told Clayton Moore to cease appearing as their licensed character. They had looked the other way for a number of years even though Moore was earning money for personal appearances as "The Lone Ranger" in full costume. While Moore could legally make appearances sans costume as Clayton Moore, the actor who played the Lone Ranger, by appearing in costume he was infringing on the Wrather Corporation's trademark. Clayton Moore never owned the Lone Ranger but had been employed to play the character on films and television. Legally the Wrather Corporation could have acted years earlier than they did. When they enjoined Moore from wearing the

mask, a furor resulted which erupted with more heat than light. Moore took the Jack Wrather Corporation to court and lost when a temporary restraining order was served on the actor in 1979. While Wrather was right and Moore was wrong, it was handled very poorly by the company. The case was t ried in the press and there big business never wins when pitted against the little guy. They were picking on the Lone Ranger! Moore even appeared on the TV program REAL PEOPLE on February 24, 1980 to take his case to the public. The studio audience was clearly on his side. Both Warner Brothers and the Wrather Corp. had miscalculated on what to them was a simple and obvious action against a copyright infringement. By stripping the Lone Ranger of his mask, a wave of resentment against the not yet released motion picture began. When THE LEGEND OF THE LONE RANGER was released in 1981, it flopped. Whether boycotts and bad feelings regarding the handling of the Clayton Moore incident contributed to its failure can't be determined, but it certainly couldn't have helped. But without star power such as Clint East-

> *The theme song for the Lone Ranger television seris was The William Tell Overture originally written by G. Rossini in 1829, years before the series is set.*

wood, Westerns have fared notoriously poorly at the boxoffice for over two decades. Even the remarkable SILVERADO, one of the finest Westerns made in the past fifty years, failed to draw audiences when released in 1985.

In 1984, following the death of Jack Wrather, the restraining order against Moore was lifted. Some time later, the rights to the Lone Ranger, Lassie and Sgt. Preston were sold for $10 million to the Southbrook Television Corporation. In 1987 Southbrook was taken over for $30 million by Palladium Entertainment, and Clayton Moore, at 75, is still the Lone Ranger. He most recently appeared as the host of the Rhino Video releases of original LONE RANGER TV episodes, introducing each with a bit of Lone Ranger lore.

While Clayton Moore is best known as the television Lone Ranger, John Hart interrupted his run for two years, playing the Ranger from 1952 until 1954, for two seasons.

The Lone Ranger Television Episode Guide

(Special thanks to Ron Vivian and John Field)

30 minute Western, ABC-TV
FIRST TELECAST: September 15, 1949
LAST TELECAST: September 12, 1961
Black and white from September 1949 to September 1955
Color from September 1956 to September 1957

SERIES SCHEDULE

Sept. 1949-Sept. 1950: Episodes 1-52 (Star: Clayton Moore)

Sept. 1950-March 1951: Episodes 52-78 (#78: last Moore)

March 1951-Sept. 1952: Episodes 1-78 rerun

Sept. 1952-Sept. 1953: Episodes 79-130 (#79: first John Hart)

Sept. 1953-Sept. 1954: Episodes 79-130 rerun (#130: last Hart)

Sept. 1954-Sept. 1955: Episodes 131-182 (#131: Moore returns)

Sept. 1955-Sept. 1956: Episodes 131-182 rerun (#182: last black and white)

Sept. 1956-Sept. 1957: Episodes 183-221 (#183: first color Lone Ranger)

Sept. 1957-Sept. 1961: Episodes 1-78, 131-221 rerun

CAST AND CREDITS

Produced by Jack Chertok Productions, Inc. (1949-54)

Produced by Jack Wrather Corp. (1954-57) under the umbrella designation "The Lone Ranger, Inc."

THE LONE RANGER
(1949-52, 1954-57):
Clayton Moore

THE LONE RANGER
(1952-54):
John Hart

TONTO: Jay Silverheels
DAN REID, JR.: Chuck Courtney
 (occasional appearances)
OPENING ANNOUNCER:
 Fred Foy (from radio show)
RANGER'S VOICE IN TITLE SEQUENCE:
 Earle Graser (from radio)
COMMERCIAL BREAK AND CLOSING ANNOUNCER (early years): Gerald Mohr
ORIGINAL SPONSOR:
 Merita Bread
MAIN THEME:
 "The William Tell Overture" composed by G. Rossini in 1829

FIRST SEASON (Episodes 1-52)

GUEST STARS (Episodes 1-3): Tris Coffin, George J. Lewis, Walter Sande, Lee Roberts, Ralph Littlefield, Frank Fenton, Glenn Strange, George Chesboro, Guy Wilkerson, Kansas Moehring, Jack Clifford, John Day

1) "Enter The Lone Ranger" (First telecast 9/15/49)
Six Texas Rangers. . . . well, you know the story. The Butch Cavendish gang ambushes the Rangers and Tonto finds the sole survivor, who adopts the identity of the Lone Ranger. He and Tonto then proceed to track down the guide who led the Rangers into the deadly ambush.

70

2) "The Lone Ranger Fights On" (9/22/49)

Tonto and the Lone Ranger confront Collins, the treacherous guide, who kindly falls to his death, leaving the Ranger's hands clean. Then they proceed to find the silver for the Ranger's bullets and a horse of the same name. But when they track down the Cavendish gang, things don't go as swimmingly.

3) "The Lone Ranger Triumphs" (9/29/49)

Justice prevails as the Lone Ranger and Tonto capture Butch Cavendish and the gang and clap them behind bars. Now it's time to fight for law and order in the early West and give strangers a bad turn by wearing a mask.

4) "The Legion Of Old Timers" (10/6/49)

When a tenderfoot from back east is hoodwinked by new ranch hands who plan to cheat him out of his property, the Ranger rounds up the old ranch hands to roust the outlaws.
GUEST STARS: Lane Bradford, Deforest Kelley, Emmett Lynn, Norman Willis, William Fawcett, Sandy Sanders

5) "Rustler's Hideout" (10/13/49)

When the outlaw, Pete Madden, is captured by ranchers, his gang retaliates by kidnapping the son of one of the ranchers. The Ranger joins the gang in order to rescue the boy and bring the outlaws to justice.
GUEST STARS: Harry Lauter, Edmund Cobb, Frank Fenton, Kay Morley, Joseph Crehan, Dick Jones, Stanley Blyston, Fred Kohler Jr., Tex Cooper

6) "War Horse" (10/20/49)

When Tonto and an Indian boy are captured as part of a plot to steal Chief Lame Bear's famous war horse, The Lone Ranger must go up against the avaricious hunter, Madrigo, to appease the angry Indian chief.
GUEST STARS: Chief Yowlachie, Leonard Fenn, Edward Cassidy, Jean DeBriac, John Merton, John Cason, Emory Parnell

7) "Pete And Pedro" (10/27/49)

The Lone Ranger convinces the shiftless Pete and Pedro to help a young girl whose neighbor is trying to cheat her out of her ranch.
GUEST STARS: Don Diamond, Shiela Ryan, John Parrish, Sandy Sanders, Rufe Davis, Bill Lester, Fred Graham

8) "The Renegades" (11/3/49)

The Lone Ranger discovers a plan by a group of Army deserters and a corrupt Indian agent to kill Tonto and his friend Chief Swift Eagle.
GUEST STARS: Lane Chandler, Ralph Moody, Harry Harvey Sr., Wheaton Chambers, Kenneth MacDonald, Gene Roth, Michael Ross, Chuck Roberson

9) "The Tenderfeet" (11/10/49)

When the Larabee brothers strike it rich, they're framed for murder and claim-jumping until the Lone Ranger uncovers the real killer.
GUEST STARS: Monte Blue, Rand Brooks, Hank Worden, Ross Ford, Ray Bennett

10) "High Heels" (11/17/49)

Pt St. Ives, the owner of the Flying M ranch, wears elevator shoes due to his sensitivity about his height. Monk Gow capitalizes on this to stir up trouble until the Lone Ranger shows that the measure of a man has nothing to do with his height.

GUEST STARS: Michael Whalen, Stanley Andrews, Jerome Sheldon, Eric Alden, Johnny Berkes

11) "Six Gun Legacy" (11/24/49)

When outlaws ambush one Bob Walker in order to impersonate him, the Lone Ranger and Tonto are tipped to the plan when they find the real Walker who'd been left for dead.

GUEST STARS: Don Haggerty, James Hickman, Ian Wolfe, Jimmy Dundee, Hal Price, Chuck Roberson

12) "Return Of The Convict" (12/1/49)

When a man who had been wrongly convicted is released after serving his prison sentence, he searches for the truth behind his accusers. When one of them turns up dead, it's up to the Lone Ranger to unmask the real criminal.

GUEST STARS: John Kellogg, Robert Emmett Keane, Chuck Roberson, Steve Clark, John Day, George Lloyd

13) "Finders Keepers" (12/8/49)

Nat Parker had been forced by the villainous Vic Crowley and Wade Turner into robbing a bank. But when he returns for the money, the Lone Ranger has to step in and save Nat's life and prevent him from being sent back to prison.

GUEST STARS: Arthur Franz, Keith Richards, Pedro DeCorddoba, David Leonard, Carol Thurston, Francis MacDonald, Robert Kellard

14) "The Masked Rider" (12/15/49)

Someone wearing a mask has been abusing the privilege and calling himself the Lone Ranger. When he kills someone, the real masked rider of the plains has to clear himself and bring the phoney masked man to justice.

GUEST STARS: Nan Leslie, Nolan Leary, Ed Rand, John Alvin, John Doucette, George Slocum, Margarita Martin

15) "Old Joe's Sister" (12/22/49)

Old Joe has been planning to finally see a long lost sister whom he's never met. When crooks try to kill off Joe so as to impersonate him and gain his expected wealth, the Lone Ranger discovers the scheme when he finds the injured man who's been left for dead. But when the outlaws get the drop on the Lone Ranger and Joe, it takes a shotgun wielded by Joe's sister to bring things under control.

GUEST STARS: Anne O'Neal, Clancy Cooper, Wade Crosby, Lester Sharpe, Joel Friedkin

16) "Cannonball McKay" (12/29/49)

Doc and Porky plan to blow up the jail in order to kill Clem Jones, whom they've framed for robbery. But Clem's best friend is Cannonball McKay, a female stagecoach driver who pretends to be a man. When the Lone Ranger becomes involved, things really become complicated.

GUEST STARS: Tris Coffin, Louise Lorimer, Mac Williams, Leonard Strong, Ralpg Peters, Charles Meredith, Fred Murray

17) "The Man Who Came Back" (1/5/50)

The Lone Ranger and Tonto help their friend Joe Crawford, who's on the verge of becoming another victim of that epidemic of trying to cheat people out of their ranch.

GUEST STARS: Emmett Lynn, Martha Hyer, Ray Gordon, Robert Wilke, Bob Carson

18) "Outlaw Town" (1/12/50)
Jack Burke has a place where crooks can hide out safely called Outlaw Town. His wife is an innocent bystander, though, and finally helps the Lone Ranger capture her husband and his guests.

GUEST STARS: Gene Reynolds, Greta Gradstedt, Bob Woodward, Marshall Bradford, John Eldredge, Ken Terrell, Robert Kellard

19) "Greed For Gold" (1/19/50)
When an old friend of Tonto and the Lone Ranger is killed from ambush, a plot to control a mine is uncovered and a secret panel in the home of a respected rancher is the clue to the killer.

GUEST STARS: Margaret Field, Kermit Maynard, Lane Bradford, Kenneth Duncan, Tudor Owen, Duke York

20) "Man Of The House" (1/26/50)
When a hen-pecked husband helps the Lone Ranger capture a gang of outlaws, life at the old homestead is never the same again.

GUEST STARS: Lane Chandler, Stanley Farrar, Dick Curtis, Tim Graham, John McGuire, William Tannen, Esther Somers

21) "Barnaby Boggs, Esquire" (2/2/50)
An old friend of the Lone Rangers named Boggs turns up in town and reveals that he can identify an outlaw named Kruger. Since Kruger has a good thing going in

town, he plots to get rid of Boggs until the Lone Ranger steps in.

GUEST STARS: Hal Price, Robert Keller, Holly Bane, Robert Strange, Bill Kennedy, Gene Roth, Nelson Leigh

22) "Sheep Thieves" (2/9/50)
Dan Reid changes places with the grandson of a wealthy sheep rancher, Dan is kidnapped and must be rescued by Tonto and the Lone Ranger.

GUEST STARS: Chuck Courtney, John Day, Bob Woodward, Pedro DeCoroba, Ross Conway, Jimmy Ogg, Harry Cording

23) "Jim Tyler's Past" (2/16/50)
Jim Tyler must prove to the Lone Ranger whether he's an honest man or a murderer.

GUEST STARS: Rand Brooks, Ray Bennett, House Peters Jr., Peter Mamakos

24) "The Man With Two Faces" (2/23/50)
When three banks owned by Joshua Blaine are robbed, the Lone Ranger and Tonto trace the crimes back to one of Blaine's nephews, but which one?

GUEST STARS: Earl Hodgins, Christian Drake, Stanley Andrews, Mira McKinney, Steven Clark

25) "Buried Treasure" (3/2/50)
When Roy Foster's outlaw brother breaks out of prison, he terrorizes Roy and his wife and steals the money they were going to use to pay off their mortgage. It takes the wiles and trickery of the Lone Ranger to capture the crook and save the farm.

GUEST STARS: David Bruce, Gail Davis, William Challee, Robert Keller, William Gould

26) "Troubled Waters" (3/9/50)
Emmy Bryson wants to cheat Dave Tucker out of his ranch to get the oil on his property. When she resorts to murder, the Lone Ranger brings her to justice.
GUEST STARS: Harry Lauter, Richard Alexander, Luther Crockett, Byron Floger, Ulla Morgan

27) "Gold Train" (3/16/50)
When the Lone Ranger is mistaken for a masked outlaw known as "The Dude" and thrown in jail, he has to escape and expose the real culprit behind the crimes.
GUEST STARS: DeForest Kelley, Billy Bletcher, Frank Fenton, John Cason, Robert Keller, Erville Anderson, Bob Woodward, Hank Peterson

28) "Pay Dirt" (3/23/50)
Claim jumpers try to get the best of the Lone Ranger, but he manages to outwit them and stop a robbery and a murder.
GUEST STARS: George J. Lewis, Martin Milner, Don Murray, Emmett Lynn, Walter Sande, Peter Lynn

29) "Billie The Great" (3/30/50)
Outlaws plan to rob the safe of a burly lady barber until the Lone Ranger steps in to thwart their plans.
GUEST STARS: Minerva Urecal, Matt McHugh, Ward Blackburn, James Flavin, Bob Woodard, George Meader, Steve Clark

30) "Never Say Die" (4/6/50)
Butch Cavendish, the man who brought the Lone Ranger into being when he ambushed the six Texas Rangers (Hi-Yo! Hi-Yo!) kidnaps the wardens son and breaks out of jail. Then they release Matt Dooley, Butch's number one boy, and trail him.

GUEST STARS: Glenn Strange, David Holt, Marjorie Eaton, Joseph Crehan, Ray Teal, Cecil Spooner, Lee Phelps

31) "Gold Fever" (4/13/50)
The Lone Ranger and Tonto deal with Ox Martin and his gang who plan to jump a valuable gold claim.
GUEST STARS: Elaine Riley, Francis Ford, George Lloyd, Harold Goodwin, Leonard Strong, John Doucette, John A. Butler, Bob Woodward

32) "Death Trap" (4/20/50)
Three deputies disappear while escorting prisoners between Petersville and Abilene. When the Lone Ranger and Tonto trace the missing men to the cabin of an old prospector then find that killers come in all disguises.
GUEST STARS: James Griffith, Lucean Littlefield, Kenneth Duncan, Lee Shumway, Jeff York, Bob Woodward, Steven Clark

33) "Matter Of Courage" (4/27/50)
A timid barber helps the Lone Ranger and Tonto entrap Dimple Hinshaw and Soapy Farrel, two murderers planning to flee across the border and escape justice.
GUEST STARS: James Arness, Don Haggerty, Edmund Cobb, Juan Duval, Raymond Largay, Dick Curtis

34) "Rifles And Renegades" (5/4/50)
The daughter of Major Mattox is in love with Lt. Haines, but when Haines is accused of supplying Army rifles to the Indians, all seems lost. Tonto investigates how Gray Hawk is getting the rifles, and when he's captured it's up to

the Lone Ranger to untangle the treacherous doings.

GUEST STARS: John Hart, I. Stanford Jolley, Russ Coglin, Robert Bice, Gene Roth, Robert Kent, Frank Marlowe, Billy Ward

35) "Bullets For Ballots" (5/11/50)

In the town of Waynesville, a man named Knox has a gang determined that their boss will win the upcoming election for mayor, and thereby control the town. But they have reckoned without the Lone Ranger and Tonto.

GUEST STARS: Craig Stevens, Marjorie Lord, John Alvin, Fredric Tozere, Ward Blackburn, Frank Jacquet, Phil Tead, Holly Bane

36) "The Black Hat" (5/18/50)

When bandits steal 200 pounds of gold, they seem to have covered their tracks so well that even the Lone Ranger can't find their trail, but he does find a crucial clue in the form of a black hat!

GUEST STARS: Jeff York, George Pembroke, John Eldredge, William Ruhl, Ed Hinton

37) "Devil's Pass" (5/25/50)

The Lone Ranger uncovers a clever frame-up involving a bank robbery when he encounters two men with bright red hair.

GUEST STARS: Jim Bannon, Jimmy Lloyd, Gene Evans, Marshall Bradford, Jed Dooley

38) "Spanish Gold" (6/1/50)

A man who was framed for murder is facing execution and so smuggles out secret information to his daughter about the location of hidden gold buried beneath the old stone prison. When the crooks who framed her father discover this, they take the girl and her boyfriend prisoner to force the secret

from them, until the Lone Ranger sets things right again.

GUEST STARS: Gail Davis, Bruce Hamilton, Kenneth Tobey, Ross Ford, Steve Clark

39) "Damsels In Distress" (6/8/50)

The Lone Ranger disguises himself as an old Rebel soldier to save three young women from a deadly European criminal.

GUEST STARS: John Banner, Tom Tyler, Phyllis Kennedy, Phil Tead, Gloria Winters

40) "Man Without A Gun" (6/15/50)

It's trouble between homesteaders and Indians and the Lone Ranger and Tonto are caught in the middle

GUEST STARS: Dick Jones, James Harrison, Robert Kellard, Eddie Dunn, House Peters Jr., Ralph Moody

41) "Pardon For Curley" (6/22/50)

An outlaw named Curley is out of jail and he's gunning for the men who put him there—the Lone Ranger and Tonto!

GUEST STARS: Douglas Kennedy, Paul Hogan, Marion Marin, Richard Alexander, John Cliff, Stephen Chase, Harry Harvey Sr., Earl Hodgins

42) "Eye For An Eye" (6/29/50)

The Lone Ranger and Tonto must protect the daughter of the governor from the vengeful outlaw Stark Durfee.

GUEST STARS: I. Stanford Jolley, Dorothy Newman, Sue England, John Cason, Chris Pin Martin, John Day, Steve Clark, David McMahon

43) "Outlaw Of The Plains" (7/6/50)

Sheriff Lem Shattuck seems like the upstanding sort, but he moonlights as a cattle rustler and obstructs attempts to solve the crimes until the Lone Ranger steps in.

GUEST STARS: Jack Lee, Edward Cassidy, Bernie Marcus, Steve Dunhill, Bert Arnold, Jay Morley, Stanley Blystone

44) "White Man's Magic" (7/13/50)

Ira Boles wants to start an Indian uprising and murders the peace-loving Chief White Eagle, blaming it on an artist. The Lone Ranger and Tonto try to intervene but find that the Indians are hell-bent on revenge.

GUEST STARS: Bill Kennedy, Pierre Watkin, Charles Stevens, Lane Bradford, Ralph Moody

45) "Trouble For Tonto" (7/20/50)

Buck Fargo kidnaps the banker's son and has Black Eagle keep him hidden. The boy is rescued, but The Lone Ranger and Tonto are almost undone when Tonto masquerades as Black Eagle in order to infiltrate Buck Fargo's outlaw gang.

GUEST STARS: Lyle Talbot, Gene Roth, Byron Folger, Russ Conklin, Robert Arthur, Bill Ward, Jimmy Dundee

46) "Sheriff Of Gunstock" (7/27/50)

This time it's the son of the sheriff of Gunstock who is kidnapped so that Rocky Hanford can continue his protection racket uninterrupted. The Lone Ranger and Tonto step in but Rocky is ready to use deadly force to protect his operation.

GUEST STARS: John Hart, Tom Irish, Walter Sande, William Vincent, John Doucette, Jack Kenny, Mira McKinney

47) "The Wrong Man" (8/3/50)

Everyone in town believes that John Meredith is guilty of murder, everyone that is except for the Lone Ranger!

GUEST STARS: Richard Crane, Glenn Vernon, Don Beddoe, Almira Sessions, Nan Leslie, Ted Adams, Paul Maxey, Walter Shumway

48) "The Beeler Gang" (8/10/50)

Another sheriff's son is kidnapped, this time by Stan Beeler and his gang, in order to force his resignation. The Lone Ranger disguises himself as a discredited doctor in order to play on the gang's fear of typhoid.

GUEST STARS: Robert Rockwell, Fred Graham, Hugh Prosser, George Slocum, William Haade, Tim Graham, Beverly Campbell, B.G. Norman, Ralph Peters

49) "The Star Witness" (8/17/50)

The only witness to a murder is twelve-year-old Johnnie Williams (whose descendant will score the music for science fiction films), but no one will listen to the boy until the Lone Ranger and Tonto force the killers out into the open.

GUEST STARS: Michael Chapin, Robert Keller, Ray Bennett, Sarah Padden, Gene Evans, Clarence Straight, Charles Watts, William Veddar, Henry Rowland

50) "The Black Widow" (8/24/50)

The Lone Ranger is able to solve a murder and recover thousands of dollars just from the clues he pieces together from a dead man's vest and a phony archaeologist.

GUEST STARS: Lane Chandler, Holly Bane, John Alvin, Nacho Galindo, Michael Whalen, George Pembroke, Peter Mamakos

51) "The Whimsical Bandit" (8/31/50)

The masked rider of the plains uses a special ring and a bull whip to undo Juan Branco and his gang.

GUEST STARS: Chuck Courtney, John Cliff, Nestor Paiva, William Ruhl, Shiela Ryan, Norman Willis, Wally West, Bud Osborne

52) "Double Jeopardy" (9/7/50)

A judge's daughter is abducted (he didn't have any sons) by Ma Hinshaw to try to force the acquittal of her son, Clyde, who's about to be tried for murder. When the Ranger and Tonto pose as crooks and break Clyde out of jail, they find more trouble waiting when they track down Ma and the judge's daughter.

GUEST STARS: Marin Sais, James Kirkwood, Jack Higram, Douglas Wood, Robert Kellard, Riley Hill, Christine Larson, Rick Roman, Brad Slaven

SEASON TWO (EPISODES 53-78)

53) "Million Dollar Wallpaper" (9/14/50)

An old man has been using what he thinks is worthless stock as wallpaper in his shack. But the mine that issued the stock has struck a new vein and the paper is suddenly valuable. The old man won't sell it, though, and so crooks kidnap him. Is that the sound of a white horse I hear?

GUEST STARS: Emmett Lynn, Lucean Littlefield, Kim Spaulding, Paul Fix, Edmund Cobb, Duke York

54) "Mission Bells" (9/21/50)

The clues mount up in the form of two mission bells, the body of a crooked land speculator and the missing page of a journal as the Lone Ranger and Tonto step in.

GUEST STARS: Tris Coffin, James Griffith, Hal Baylor, Walter Sande, Rosa Turich, Lee Roberts

55) "Dead Man's Chest" (9/28/50)

Because an old prospector carries a wooden chest with him where ever he goes, crooks suspect it contains gold and kill the man for it. But all they get for their trouble is a confrontation with the Lone Ranger.

GUEST STARS: Harry Lauter, Stephen Chase, Frank Sully, Myron Healy, Ray Montgomery, William Veddar, George Lloyd

56) "Outlaws Revenge" (10/5/51)

When the Lone Ranger provides the evidence which sends one of the Trigger Taylor gang to the gallows, they plot retribution. The Ranger doesn't yet know upstanding banker Calvin Blair is really Trigger Taylor himself!

GUEST STARS: Larry Blake, Richard Bailey, William Heade, Richard Beach, Kenneth MacDonald, Steven Clark, Larry Johns

57) "Danger Ahead" (10/12/50)

The Lone Ranger and Tonto rely on the help of Boswell the ventriloquist who witnessed the murder of sheriff Roberts at the hands of the outlaw named Hatch.

GUEST STARS: Max Terhune, William Green, Holly Bane, Don Haggerty, Jack Briggs

58) "Crime In Time" (10/19/50)

The Lone Ranger and Tonto track down the Watkins brothers

and the counterfeiting jeweler who killed one of the brothers and then went into partnership with the other!

GUEST STARS: Monte Blue, Lane Bradford, Fred Libby, A. Butler

59) "Drink Of Water" (10/26/50)
Crooks pretending to be rainmakers prey on the parched town of Greenville and even plan to kill the Lone Ranger and Tonto before they hit the trail.

GUEST STARS: Bill Kennedy, Stanley Andrews, Linda Johnson, Mickey Simpson, Gregg Barton, Arthur Stone, Harlan Briggs, Mitchell Kowal

60) "Thieves Money" (11/2/50)
A counterfeiter named Dumont has already killed a government agent to mask his crimes and when he thinks that the Lone Ranger and Tonto are on to him he decides they they're next on his hit list.

GUEST STARS: David McMahon, John Doucette, Jack Briggs, Charles Watts, Ward Blackburn

61) "The Squire" (11/9/50)
Amos Carter sees the face of one of the men who hold up the bank. Although shot, Amos escapes. The Lone Ranger steps in to expose the crooks, including the secret mastermind behind the robbers.

GUEST STARS: Margaret Kerry, Robert Wilke, John Cliff, Peter George Lynn, Hugh Prosser, Steve Dunhill, Alex Sharp

62) "Masked Deputy" (11/16/50)
Aging lawman Sheriff Higgins teams up with the Lone Ranger to bring down wealthy businessman Will Bradley and his gang of rustlers.

GUEST STARS: Lane Chandler, Edmund Cobb, Dave Willock, Bert Arnold, Peter Mamakos, Stuart Randall, Carol Thurston, Gregg Rogers

63) "Bankers Choice" (11/23/50)
Three blackmailers convince banker Henry McFarland that his son, Andrew, is a thief. But the Lone Ranger and Tonto expose the scheme and clear Andrew of any wrong-doing.

GUEST STARS: David Bruce, John Merton, Mickey Simpson, Bud Osborne, Phillis Morris, Commander Murray, Jack Mower

64) "Desert Adventure" (11/30/50)
The Lone Ranger and Tonto trail the Yuma Kid through bad desert country and nearly succumb to the ordeal before capturing the ruthless outlaw.

GUEST STARS: House Peters Jr., Holly Bane, Lane Bradford, Lee Shumway, Charles Horvath, Kermit Maynard

65) "Bad Medicine" (12/7/50)
The Lone Ranger and Tonto track a wounded robber and his partner to the home of a doctor who is being forced to help the crooks.

GUEST STARS: Dick Curtis, Sandy Sanders, Robert Kellard, Greta Gransstedt, Hal Fieberling, Bob Carson, Harry Harvey Sr., James Guildfoyle

66) "One Jump Ahead" (12/14/50)
Two confidence men go around defrauding the parents of Civil War soldiers until the Lone Ranger and Tonto smash their racket.

GUEST STARS: Robert Rockwell, Nolan Leary, Richard Crane, Dorothy Vaugh, John Eldredge

67) "Lady Killer" (12/21/50)

Lela Anson is a clever actress pretending to be in love with Sheriff John Markum while she and her two helpers secretly commit successful robberies and murders. Only the Lone Ranger can prove the truth to the sheriff in time.

GUEST STARS: Robert Kent, Ray Montgomery, Fred Libby, Bill Vincent, I. Stanford Jolley, Nan Leslie, Russell Trent

68) "Paid In Full" (12/28/50)

The man who holds the mortgage on Jim Craig's Bar-C Ranch wants it for himself and will stop at nothing to get it, until the Lone Ranger uncovers the scheme.

GUEST STARS: Harry Lauter, John Day, Emmett Lynn, Wanda McKay, Larry Blake, Charles Watts

69) "Letter Of The Law" (1/4/51)

Sam Slater capitalizes on his former friendship with a man who's now gone straight in order to hide out on his farm. But with the Lone Ranger's help, Jeff Niles isn't taken advantage of for long.

GUEST STARS: Warren Douglas, Monte Blue, Noel Neil, Ed Hinton, Douglas Henderson, Douglas Wood

70) "The Silent Voice" (1/11/51)

A woman who cannot write or talk is the only one who can solve three cold-blooded murders, with the Lone Ranger's help.

GUEST STARS: Ross Ford, Mike Ragan, Christine Larson, John Morgan, Mira McKinney, Hal Fieberling

71) "The Outcast" (1/18/51)

The Texas Rangers set a trap by pretending that one of their own has gone bad in order to trap a gang of robbers and killers. Little do they know how much they have in common with the Lone Ranger.

GUEST STARS: Robert Rockwell, Lane Bradford, Mickey Simpson, Pierre Watkin, Edmund Cobb, Fred Libby, Stephen Chase, Denver Pyle, Gregg Barton, Bob Woodward

72) "Backtrail" (1/25/51)

When the Lone Ranger and Tonto discover that white men have been masquerading as Indians, they reveal this to Walter Mason, unaware that he's the man behind the scheme.

GUEST STARS: Rex Lease Kim Spaulding, Robert Bice, Riley Hill, Herbert Lytton, Bud Osborne

73) "Behind The Law" (2/1/51)

When a gang lives peaceably in one country and terrorizes another, it's up to the Lone Ranger and Tonto to help the authorities trap the tricky outlaws.

GUEST STARS: Gene Evans, George Cheseboro, Marshall Bradford, Gene Roth, James Guildfoyle, Bob Carson, Ward Blackburn, Clarence Straight

74) "Trouble At Black Rock" (2/8/51)

An old prospector finds the loot of an outlaw who's just broken out of prison, and who wants his money at any price.

GUEST STARS: George J. Lewis, Wanda McKay, Michael Ansara, John Alvin, Emmett Lynn, Constance Purdy

75) "Two Gold Lockets" (2/15/51)

The Lone Ranger is able to save a boy from the life of crime and mend the relationship between the boy and his father.

GUEST STARS: Darryl Hickman, Dwayne Hickman, Stanley Andrews, Tom Powers, John Cliff, Ben Welden, Greta Granstadt, Duke York

76) "The Hooded Men" (2/22/51)

By using the same disguise employed by a gang of robbers and killers, the Lone Ranger is able to bring them to justice.

GUEST STARS: Mira McKinney, Denver Pyle, John Doucette, Walter Sande, Lane Bradford, Morte Thompson

77) "Friend In Need" (3/1/51)

The Lone Ranger trails killer Luke Banner in order to bring him to justice and save an innocent man from the gallows.

GUEST STARS: John McGuire, Edmund Cobb, David Leonard, Stephen Clark, Gail Davis, Joe Domingues, Robert Bice, Paul Fierro, Salvador Barquez, Ed Clark

78) "Mr. Trouble" (3/8/51)

In order for Rick Merill to keep his franchise, the Lone Ranger and Tonto have to help him complete a railroad.

GUEST STARS: Jim Bannon, House Peters Jr., Larry Blake, Harry Harvey Sr., Russell Trent, Robert Rockwell, Paul Campbell, Robert Kellard, Earl Hodgins, David McMahon

SEASON THREE (Episodes 79-130)

79) "Outlaw's Son" (9/11/52)

When an outlaw is released from prison, his own son plans to kill him until the Lone Ranger steps in to prove that the man has reformed and bring his family back together

again.

GUEST STARS: Robert Rockwell, Bob Arthur, Irene Vernon, Paul Fierro, William Haade, John Pickard

80) "Outlaw Underground" (9/18/52)

When a cynical reporter from back east plans to write an expose on the Lone Ranger, he gets in over his head with a gang of outlaws and the subject of his article ends up rescuing the reporter from certain death.

GUEST STARS: Robert Clark, John Downey, Dick Reeves, Michael Ansara, James Parnell, Lois Hal, Lester Dorr

81) "Special Edition" (9/25/52)

The Lone Ranger captures a gang of outlaws who try to stop the publisher of a small newspaper from printing the truth about them.

GUEST STARS: Judd Holdren, Victor Sutherland, Larry Blake, Hal K. Dawson, Nan Leslie, Marshall Ruth, John Close

82) "Desperado At Large" (10/2/52)

The Lone Ranger and Tonto rescue a secret agent from a lynch mob.

The man is masquerading as an outlaw in order to capture the real criminal.

GUEST STARS: Lee Van Cleef, Robert Filmer, Steve Clark, Douglas Kennedy, James Brown

83) "Through The Wall" (10/9/52)

Old Toby helps the Lone Ranger capture a criminal in order to ease his conscience. When he'd helped build the prison years ago he left a secret exit in the wall.

GUEST STARS: Dabbs Greer, Douglas Evans, George Slocum,

Phil Tead, Holly Bane, Monte Blue, Raymond Largay

84) "Jeb's Gold Mine" (10/16/52)

The Lone Ranger keeps a homesteader from being cheated out of his land by people who know there is gold on it.

GUEST STARS: Raymond Greenleaf, Robert Bray, Syd Saylor, Lane Bradford, Rory Mallison, Stephen Chase, B.G. Norman

85) "Frame For Two" (10/23/52)

A young rancher is framed for murder and it looks like he'll hang for the crime until the Lone Ranger uncovers the real culprit.

GUEST STARS: Bob Livingston, Richard Crane, John Damler, James Parnell, Robert B. Williams

86) "Ranger In Danger" (10/30/52)

A killer tricks a boy into leading the Lone Ranger and Tonto into a trap where the outlaw plans to betray the boy and kill all three of his potential victims.

87) "Delayed Action" (11/6/52)

The Lone Ranger and Tonto track down Flint Taylor and his gang after a long search and expose the cover they'd been operating under.

GUEST STARS: James Griffith, Sailor Vincent, Stanley Andrews, Franklyn Farnum, Ben Welden

88) "The Map" (11/13/52)

When crooks steal a map in order to learn what land is going to be purchased by the railroad, the Lone Ranger manages to outwit the felons with the help of a 13 year old chemistry wiz.

GUEST STARS: Lanny Rees, Frank Wilcox,, Steve Darrell, Har-

lan Warde, Geraldine Wall

89) "Trial By Fire" (11/20/52)

The Lone Ranger proves that a feuding son did not shoot his father and, with the help of the young man's wife, is able to mend the family rift.

GUEST STARS: Pierre Watkin, Gail Davis, Marshall Bradford, Robert Wilke, Ross Ford, Ralpg Peters, Stanley Andrews, Emerson Tracy, Mickey Simpson

90) "The Pledge" (11/27/52)

A phony letter about a young man's supposedly ill mother causes the sheriff to release the boy temporarily with the promise that he'll return in time for his trial. The young man was framed for the crime he's accused of , though, and the real crooks plan to kill him off before the truth comes out.

GUEST STARS: Ross Elliott, Lee Phelps, Sam Flint, Harry Chesshire, Hayden Rorke, Wanda McKay, David McMahon

91) "Treason At Dry Creek" (12/4/52)

Men working at a remote Pony Express outpost are selling army plans to the Indians and only the swift action of the Lone Ranger can avert a massacre.

GUEST STARS: Frank Fenton, Rand Brooks, Ann Doran, Robert Carson, Paul Fierro, Charles Evans, Britt Wood

92) "The Condemned Man" (12/11/52)

When an Indian is murdered, an innocent man is framed for the crime and is sentenced to hang in a speedy trial in order to avert an Indian uprising. Only the Lone Ranger can clear the man in time.

GUEST STARS: Don Beddoe, Monte Blue, Russel Hicks, Rusty

Westcoat, Maurice Jara, Charles Gibb, Myron Healey

93) "The New Neighbor" (12/18/52)

When a new settler in the region becomes involved with other ranchers in a battle over water rights, it's up to the Lone Ranger to straighten everything out.

GUEST STARS: Walter Sande, B.G. Norman, Edward Clark, Robert Forrest, Barbara Woodell, Larry Hudson, John Phillips, John Alvin

94) "Best Laid Plans" (12/25/52)

A gang plans to get one of their number elected sheriff and thereby control the region, and only the Lone Ranger and Tonto can smash their deadly scheme.

GUEST STARS: Judd Holdren, House Peters Jr., John Pickard, Cathy Downs, Ralph Sanford, John Bryant

95) "Indian Charlie" (1/1/53)

Only the Lone Ranger knows why an Indian boy who was raised by whites seems to have turned renegade, and things are not all that they seem.

GUEST STARS: Glenn Strange, Walter Reed, Sally Corner, Alan Wells, John Cason, Harry Harvey Sr.

96) "Empty Strong Box" (1/8/53)

A rash of stage robberies prompts lawmen to set a trap with a bomb hidden in a strongbox, but the Lone Ranger almost falls victim to the trap.

GUEST STARS: James Todd, Hugh Prosser, Don Mahin, Bud Osborne, Robert Carson, Edwin Rand

97) "Trader Boggs" (1/15/53)

When Barnaby Boggs, an old friend of the Ranger's (see episode #21) decides to settle down and open a store, his only rival in town tries to blast him out of business. But as usual the bad guys have figured without the Lone Ranger.

GUEST STARS: Hal Price, I. Stanford Jolley, Kenneth Duncan, Aline Towne, John Crawford

98) "Bandits In Uniform" (1/22/53)

When crooks pretend to be tax collectors to victimize a Spanish family, the Lone Ranger steps in to bring the outlaws to justice.

GUEST STARS: John Doucette, I. Stanford Jolley, James Parbell, Robert Bray, George Douglas, Gil Donaldson

99) "The Godless Men" (1/29/53)

The Lone Ranger proves that justice triumphs over sin when he tracks down the outlaws who robbed a young preacher of the money intended for building a church.

GUEST STARS: Hugh Beaumont, Ray Page, Hugh Sanders, Keith Richards

100) "The Devil's Bog" (2/5/53)

When a doctor wants to fill in a swamp to stop the spread of fever carried by mosquitoes, outlaws use violence to attempt to halt the endeavor as the project would uncover a body they hid in the swamp.

GUEST STARS: Harry Harvey Sr., Hugh Prosser, Ferris Taylor, Bruce Edwards, Barbara Woodell, Van DeSautels, Frank Richards

101) "Right To Vote" (2/15/53)

A town is being run by a gang of crooked officials who want to be

certain they aren't voted out of office. When the petitions calling for a special election to throw the bums out are stolen, only the Lone Ranger can find them in time to keep the wheels of democracy turning smoothly.

GUEST STARS: Douglas Kennedy, John Damler, Dick Elliott, Ben Welden, Richard Avonde

102) "The Sheriff's Son" (2/19/53)

When a sheriff's son is released from prison, he's embittered because his own father had been the one who turned him in. He's about to resume his outlaw ways when the Lone Ranger shows him the error of his ways.

GUEST STARS: Alan Wells, Claudia Barrett, Walter Bonn, Hugh Prosser, William Haade, Emerson Treacy

103) "Tumblerock Law" (2/26/53)

When an important witness against Ace Broderick is kidnapped, it's up to the Lone Ranger and Tonto bring the witness back in time to testify.

GUEST STARS: Paul Birch, Richard Crane, Kim Spaulding, Byron Folger, Tom London, Bill Slack, Steve Brodie

104) "Sinner By Proxy" (3/5/53)

A crook poses as the Lone Ranger involving the masked man in a robbery. When someone else falsely implicates the Ranger, he has his hands full proving his innocence.

GUEST STARS: Hugh Sanders, Greta Granstedit, Paul Hogan, Ross Elliott, Dee Pollock, Russ Conway, Mickey Simpson, Stephen Chase

105) "A Stage For Mademoiselle" (3/12/53)

A singer thinks the plan to steal her jewels is just a publicity stunt until the Lone Ranger has to recover the gems when the damsel realizes that she's been tricked.

GUEST STARS: Noreen Nash, Douglas Evans, Emmett Lynn, Edmund Cobb, Lane Bradford, Frank Wilcox

106) "A Son By Adoption" (3/19/53)

An adopted boy believes his real father died fighting for his country. The man is actually an outlaw who finally does die a hero's death when he takes a bullet meant for the boy's foster father.

GUEST STARS: Russ Conway, Peter Mamakos, William Challee, Frank Richards, Dennis Ross

107) "Mrs. Banker" (3/26/53)

The Lone Ranger uses his old prospector disguise to try to solve a series of stagecoach robberies but almost falls victim to the robbers himself.

GUEST STARS: Esther Somers, Steve Mitchell, Dan White, Robert Neil, Harmon Stevens

108) "Trouble In Town" (4/2/53)

A robbery causes a run on a bank and only the Lone Ranger and Tonto can find the stolen money in time to prevent the bank from failing and causing many people great personal loss.

GUEST STARS: Lyle Talbot, Mira McKinney, Ross Ford, William Fawcett, Jim Maloney, Dayton Lummis, John Cason, Fred Essler

109) "Black Gold" (4/9/53)

A young geologist is beaten up by outlaws who intend to cheat a man out of property which has oil on it. The Lone Ranger finds the injured man and puts a stop to the dastardly scheme.

GUEST STARS: Robert Shayne, Jim Hayward, Todd Karns, William Veddar

110) "The Durango Kid" (4/16/ 53)

A young lady mistakenly believes that a notorious killer is her long lost brother until the Lone Ranger is able to find her real brother and prevent her from becoming involved with the wrong crowd.

GUEST STARS: James Griffith, Nan Leslie, Judd Holdren, Lee Shumway, Pierre Watkin, Fred Libby

111) "The Deserter" (4/23/53)

A young soldier regrets deserting the Army and joins forces with the Lone Ranger to bring a band of outlaws to justice and thereby redeem himself.

GUEST STARS: Chuck Courtney, Gene Roth, Robert Foulk, John Merton, Keith Richards, Lane Bradford, Randy Brooks

112) "Embezzler's Harvest" (4/ 30/53)

Thieves steal the money earmarked for an irrigation project and murder a man to frame him for the crime and make it appear that he embezzled it. But the Lone Ranger finds clues which point to the real culprits.

GUEST STARS: Lois Hall, Harry Harvey Sr., Stephen Chase, Leonard Freeman

113) "El Toro" (5/7/53)

When Dan Reid saves the life of the bandit leader known as El Toro, the man later repays the debt when Dan, Tonto and the Lone Ranger are facing death at the hands of outlaws.

GUEST STARS: Chuck Courtney, Robert Spencer, Jim Hayward, Eugene Wesson, Richard Avone, Stan Blystone

114) "The Brown Pony" (5/14/ 53)

Tommy runs away with his pony to keep his mother from selling it to get the money she needs to buy the evidence from crooks that will prove the boy's father innocent of the crime for which he was sent to jail. When the boy is injured, the Lone Ranger finds him and sets things right again.

GUEST STARS: Lee Van Cleef, Adele Longmire, Dennis Ross, Charles Stevens

115) "Triple Cross" (5/21/53)

A young girl witnesses the murder of a man who led his friends to the loot from a Wells Fargo robbery.

GUEST STARS: Jack Ingram, John Cliff, James Todd, Judy Nugent, Joseph Haworth, Fred Coby

116) "Wake Of War" (5/28/53)

A murder is committed by gamblers who want to keep warring factions at each other's throat so as not to interfere with their operation, but the Lone Ranger uncovers the truth.

GUEST STARS: Richard Crane, Don Beddoe, Hugh Prosser, John Crawford, Sheb Wooley

117) "Death In The Forest" (6/4/ 53)

The Lone Ranger uncovers a plot to murder a territorial governor which implicates the man's aide.

GUEST STARS: DeForest Kelley, Raymond Greenleaf, Mickey Simpson

118) "Gentleman From Julesburg" (6/11/53)

The Lone Ranger convinces a reformed gambler to help him expose a gang of crooks and save a young man who turns out to be the gambler's long lost son.

GUEST STARS: Walter Reed, Nan Leslie, Eddy Waller, Robert Ned, Fred Libby, Robert Fillmore

119) "Hidden Fortune" (6/18/53)

The Lone Ranger disrupts the plot of a gang who had been released from prison after ten years only to discover that a house had been built on the spot where they buried their ill-gotten gains.

GUEST STARS: Hugh Prosser, Bruce Payne, Steve Darrell, Ann Doran, I. Stanford Jolley

120) "The Old Cowboy" (6/25/53)

The Lone Ranger saves the day when crooks attempt to cheat an old man with failing eyes out of his land which the railroad wants to buy.

GUEST STARS: Frank Fenton, Russell Simpson, Terry Frost, Steve Brodie, Denver Pyle, Bill Slack

121) "Woman From Omaha" (7/2/53)

The Lone Ranger helps a woman save her stage line from corrupt outside interests.

GUEST STARS: Minerva Urecal, Harry Harvey Sr., Charles Horvath, Terry Wilson, Hank Worden, John Cliff, John Damler

122) "Gunpowder Joe" (7/9/53)

Crooks hire an old timer to blast open a cave and get at their loot which is hidden under tons of rock.

GUEST STARS: Chubby Johnson, Stanley Blystone, Glenn Strange, Frank Richards, Mauritz Hugo, Herbert Lytton

123) "The Midnight Rider" (7/16/53)

A young man becomes an outlaw to prey on the crooks who cheated his father, but in the end it takes the Lone Ranger to save the day.

GUEST STARS: Darry Hickman, Harry Woods, Hank K. Dawson, Guy Hayclan, Steve Darrell, Harry Cheshire, Mickey Simpson

124) "Stage To Estacado" (7/23/53)

The Lone Ranger saves a young couple from ruthless competitors who don't want their new stage line to succeed.

GUEST STARS: Sheb Wooley, Monte Blue, Lee Van Cleef, Phyllis Coates, Douglas Evans, Ian MacDonald

125) "The Perfect Crime" (7/30/53)

A discredited professor uses the cover of being a schoolteacher to plot a bank robbery. When a real schoolteacher sees through him, she faces death until saved by the Lone Ranger.

GUEST STARS: Phyllis Coates, Edna Holland, Hayden Rorke, Robert Bray, Bud Osborne, Terry Frost, Richard Avone

126) "The Ghost Of Coyote Canyon" (8/6/53)

A gang uses the ruse of a ghost to frighten people away from their hideout. They kill those who aren't fooled until the Lone Ranger brings them to justice.

GUEST STARS: Lucian Littlefield, Richard Alexander, Marshall Reed, Tom London, John Pickard, Hank Worden

127) "Old Bailey" (8/13/53)

Gambles frame Old Bailey for the murder of a man who was actually killed for not paying his gambling debts. But the Lone Ranger uncovers the real killers.

GUEST STARS: Phil Tead, Bruce Cowling, Steve Pendleton, Ray Montgomery, John Crawford

128) "Prisoner In Jeopardy" (8/20/53)

A young man who served time in prison for a crime he didn't commit is kidnapped from the stage taking him home. He's about to be framed a second time until the Lone Ranger arrives on the scene.

GUEST STARS: Richard Crane, Stanley Blystone, Jerome Sheldon, Dorothy Patrick, Dick Rich, House Peters, Jr.

129) "Diamond In The Rough" (8/27/53)

When the Lone Ranger is chasing a thief through a theatre, the crook hides a diamond inside a ventriloquist's dummy while the felon continues trying to elude the masked man in the theatre.

GUEST STARS: Emory Parnell, Leo Britt, Harry Lauter, House Peters, Jr.

130) "The Red Mark" (9/3/53)

Thieves make off with a pile of loot only to discover that all of the bills are marked in red, making it difficult to use them. This eventually brings them into fateful contact with the Lone Ranger.

GUEST STARS: Frank Fenton, Paul Bryar, Tom London, Steve Roberts, Alan Wells

SEASON FOUR
(Episodes 131-182)

131) "The Fugitive" (9/9/54)

Clay Trowbridge is falsely accused of murder and breaks out of jail to escape a lynch mob. The Territorial Governor calls upon the Lone Ranger and Tonto to prove the man innocent and bring the real killers to justice.

GUEST STARS: Paul Langdon, John Doucette, Griff Barnett, Denver Pyle, Bob Woodward

132) "Ex-Marshal" (9/16/54)

A former marshal who'd packed it in and believed himself disgraced, joins forces with the Lone Ranger and Tonto to track down a notorious killer and brings his gang to justice. In so doing the marshal decides to return to his old duties.

GUEST STARS: Stanley Clements, Tyler McVey, John Cason, House Peters Jr., Ray Teal, Glenn Strange

133) "Message To Fort Apache" (9/23/54)

The Lone Ranger and Tonto help the U.S. Army to stop the illegal sale of guns to the Indians and avert more bloodshed.

GUEST STARS: Bob Livingston, Chick Chandler, Nancy Hale, Charles Meredith, Lane Bradford, Bob Woodward, Scott Elliott, Steve Brodie, Sheb Wooley, Fay Roope, Harry Harvey Sr.

134) "The Frightened Woman" (9/30/54)

After a woman witnesses a robbery, a bandit leader orders her to be killed until the Lone Ranger foils the plot.

GUEST STARS: Emlen Davies, Don Murray, Emmet Lynn, Rich-

ard Travis, Rickey Murray, Don C. Harvey, Bruce Cowling

135) "Gold Town" (10/7/54)
The Lone Ranger and Tonto manage to successfully protect a $100,000 inheritance from a phony Englishman and his treacherous schemes.
GUEST STARS: Edward Ashley, James Craven, Anthony Sydes, Pierre Watkin, Myron Healey, James Parnell, Earl Hodgins

136) "Six Gun Sanctuary" (10/14/54)
The town of Reidsville is under the thumb of killers and outlaws. When a body is found, the Lone Ranger steps in to help the local sheriff get things under control and protect his young son from the threats of the criminals.
GUEST STARS: Harry Harvey Sr., Douglas Kennedy, Frank Fenton, Hal Baylor, Don Beddoe, Robert B. Williams

137) "Outlaw's Trail" (10/21/54)
The town of Painted Post is victimized by two gunmen who set out to commit crimes designed to bring cattlemen and homesteaders into conflict. When the Lone Ranger and Tonto witness one of the cold-blooded murders, they move in to end the terror and bloodshed.
GUEST STARS: Jack Elam, Robert Bice, Christian Drake, Rory Mallinson, Robert Bray, Clarence Straight, Hugh Sanders

138) "Stage To Teshimingo" (10/28/54)
When desperadoes continually rob the stages running between the mining towns of Gunsight and Teshimingo, the Lone Ranger and Tonto move to end the rule of the highwaymen.
GUEST STARS: Don McGowan, Ben Welden, Robert Carson, Mira McKinney, Hank Worden, Kenneth Patterson, Lane Bradford, Robert Foulk

139) "Texas Draw" (11/4/54)
Dillon is a gunslinger with plans to make a killing in the field of copper mining. Standing in his way is Brother John Thorpe, a minister who owns the land which has the copper deposit and who plans to build a school for orphan boys there.
GUEST STARS: Christopher Dark, Barry Kelly, Marion Ross, Frank Richards, Joe Haworth, James Westerfield

140) "Rendezvous At Whipsaw" (11/11/54)
A band of outlaws pose as respectable citizens in the town of Whipsaw. But when a young woman witnesses them commit murder, they kidnap her brother and hold him hostage to prevent her from testifying against them. If the Lone Ranger can save her brother, the gang will go down to defeat.
GUEST STARS: John Doucette, William Haade, Don Beddoe, Hugh Sanders, Clancy Cooper, Ann O'Neal, Paul Brinegar

141) "Dan Reid's Fight For Life" (11/18/54)
When Dan Reid falls prey to a treacherous Mexican bandit, only the Lone Ranger and Tonto have a chance to save their friend's life and smoke the outlaw out from his hideout.
GUEST STARS: Chuck Courtney, John Stephenson, Henry Kulky, Mickey Simpson, Nacho Galino, Nestor Paiva

142) "Tenderfoot" (11/25/54)

When crooks try to force Mr. Ferris into selling his ranch to them through sabotage and intimidation, the Lone Ranger must step in to see that justice triumphs in the end.

GUEST STARS: Robert Horton, Hal Baylor, George Chandler, William Forrest, Martin Garralga, Dan Riss

143) "A Broken Match" (12/2/54)

Jeff Williams is jailed after a stage is robbed and people killed, largely because he's an ex-convict. When the real killers plan a robbery of the bank with the help of an accomplice, the Lone Ranger uncovers the identity of the outlaws through a trail of match sticks.

GUEST STARS: Whit Bissell, Nan Leslie, Fred Coby Phil Tead, Robert Quarry, Paul Keast, Glen Gordon, Don Harvey

144) "Colorado Gold" (12/9/54)

The Lone Ranger have to deal with a greedy reprobate and a mine tunnel loaded with dynamite before their day is done in this adventure.

GUEST STARS: Robert Shayne, Claudia Barrat, Mike Dennis, Gene Roth, Gil Donaldson, George Barrows, Norman Keats

145) "Homer With A High Hat" (12/16/54)

A dude from back east learns about the old west in the school of hard knocks while the Lone Ranger traces $200,000 in stolen gold.

GUEST STARS: Tom Brown, Kathleen Crowley, Minerva Urecal, Peter Hanson, Fred Libby, Chick Chandler, Rex Thorson, Terry Frost

146) "Two For Juan Ringo" (12/23/54)

When an Englishman gains a stranglehold on the town of Border City, the Lone Ranger takes on the guise of the outlaw Juan Ringo in order to bring the crook and his gang to justice.

GUEST STARS: John Hoyt, Lyle Talbot, John Cason, Bert Holland, Robert Bray, Dennis Moore

147) "The Globe" (12/30/54)

When the Lone Ranger and Tonto find a badly injured bank clerk at the bottom of a deserted mine shaft, they uncover a plot by the bankers of the town of Oreville to cheat the citizens out of their hard-earned savings.

GUEST STARS: Phil Tead, Greg Palmer, Frank Ferguson, Phil Chambers, Michael Whalen, Stuart Randall

148) "Dan Reid's Sacrifice" (1/6/55)

In order for the Lone Ranger and Tonto to get the goods on a gang of horse thieves, Dan has to allow his trusty horse, Victor, to be stolen.

GUEST STARS: Chuck Courtney, Percy Hilton, Fred Graham, Bill Kennedy, John Cliff, Mickey Knox

149) "Enfield Rifle" (1/13/55)

The Lone Ranger and Tonto discover that renegade Indians have gotten their hands on the new repeating Enfield rifle, smuggled in from Canada. They must join forces with the U.S. Army in order to quell this deadly threat.

GUEST STARS: Rand Brooks, Frank Ferguson, Rico Alaniz, Walter Coy, Maurice Jara, Peter Mamakos

150) "The School Story" (1/20/55)

The Lone Ranger and Tonto have to teach young Tommy Righter the importance of education when a school house is planed for construction in the area.

GUEST STARS: Lee Aaker, Stanley Andrews, John Doucette, Dick Elliott, Norman Keiths, Madge Meredith, Paul Birch

151) "The Quiet Highwayman" (1/27/55)

The town of Bakersville is being plagued by a highwayman who disguises himself with a hood and never speaks, thus causing the townspeople to eye each other suspiciously. Finally the U.S. marshal decides to summon the Lone Ranger to solve the crime wave.

GUEST STARS: Chuck Courtney, Harry Harvey Sr., Francis MacDonald, Dan Riss, Dennis King Jr., Kathryn Card, Hugh Sanders, Roger Creed

152) "The Heritage Of Treason" (2/3/55)

The cattle baron, Halstead, envisions himself as the king of Arizona and will stop at nothing, not even murder, to insure his goal. But the Lone Ranger isn't far away when injustice rules the land.

GUEST STARS: Stuart Randall, Ed Hinton, Don Haggerty, Peter Whitney, Burt Mustin, Charles Halton

153) "The Lost Chalice" (2/10/55)

When the Lone Ranger and Tonto visit the Padre of Mission Valley, they aid in finding a new water supply for the area, and in so doing encounter escaped convicts and discover a long lost golden chalice.

GUEST STARS: James Griffith, Edward Colmans, Argentia Brunetti, Joseph Turkel, William Challee, Julian Rivero

154) "Code Of The Pioneers" (2/17/55)

The town of Gold Creek is planning to elect a new sheriff, but Bradley, the local political boss, wants his own man to win, and he thinks stealing the printing press and putting out a phony newspaper slandering the honest candidate will put the election in his pocket, but he has figured without the Lone Ranger!

GUEST STARS: Walter Reed, Chuck Courtney, Bill Kennedy, Lyle Talbot, Barry Curtis, Harry Lauter, Paul Keast, Emillen Davies

155) "The Law Lady" (2/24/55)

When the young wife of an elected official steps in to fill his office after he's murdered by outlaws, the criminals try to get her out of the way as well, until the Lone Ranger and Tonto intervene.

GUEST STARS: Marjorie Lord, Richard Travis, Don Garrett, Peter Hanson

156) "Uncle Ed" (3/3/55)

An old storyteller, Uncle Ed, has spent years exaggerating the tales of his youth. But when escaped killers besiege his farm and he helps the Lone Ranger save the day, he finally has a true tale rather than a tall tale to tell.

GUEST STARS: Will Wright, June Whitley, Peter Mamakos, Frank Hagney, Nadine Ashdown, John Damler, Bruce Cowling, Ed Hinton

157) "Jornado Del Muerto" (3/10/55)

The outlaw Cantrell has lived

among Indians for many years, but the Lone Ranger and Tonto must finally find and bring the criminal to justice to pay for his many crimes, including inciting Indians to attack whites.

GUEST STARS: Richard Crane, Joseph Vitale, Rick Vallin, John Hubbard, Marshall Bradford, Steven Ritch, Raymond Meurer, Ray Montgomery

158) "Sunstroke Mesa" (3/17/55)

The Lone Ranger and Tonto prove to a youth what the best path in life is to follow when they bring a band of outlaws in to pay for their crimes.

GUEST STARS: Chuck Courtney, John Pickard, Dwayne Hickman, Joseph Crehan, John Mansfield, Don C. Harvey

159) "Sawtelle Saga's End" (3/24/55)

Aunt Maggie seems like a kindly old lady, but she's actually the ruthless leader of a band of bank robbers, and when the Lone Ranger and Tonto cross her path trying to capture the thieves, she tries to write finis to their careers by locking them in a wooden shack and setting it on fire!

GUEST STARS: Peter Hanson, Robert Foulk, Francis Bavier, Paul Keast, William Forrest

160) "The Too-Perfect Signature" (3/31/55)

When a crooked attorney and his assistant forge documents to transfer the ownership of a valuable homestead into their names, the Lone Ranger rides to the rescue.

GUEST STARS: Ray Teal, Stacey Keach, Glenn Strange, Charles Meredith, Katherine Warren, Terry Frost, Will White

161) "Trigger Finger" (4/7/55)

When the Lone Ranger stops a runaway stage, he and Dan Reid find themselves up against a vicious band of outlaws who have been terrorizing the area.

GUEST STARS: Chuck Courtney, Laura Elliott, Stacey Keach, Douglas Kennedy, Taggart Casey, Keith Richards, Mickey Simpson, Steve Dunhill

162) "The Tell-Tale Bullet" (4/14/55)

When a country doctor pulls one of the Lone Ranger's silver bullets out of a man who has been shot, the doctor and the bullet point the way to the wounded desperado.

GUEST STARS: Roy Roberts, Anthony Caruso, Dennis Weaver, Mason Allen Dinehart, John Cason

163) "False Accusations" (4/28/55)

A mysterious Night Rider has been terrorizing the town of Rock Point, and when the Lone Ranger shows up in the area, he's mistaken for the bandit.

GUEST STARS: Whit Bissell, Michael Whalen, Marshall Reed, Robert Bray, Bruce Cowling, Harry Harvey Sr.

164) "Gold Freight" (5/5/55)

When two freight lines operate in Eagle City, Jack Ronson stages a robbery and points the blame at his competitor, Sam Slater. Only the Lone Ranger, Dan Reid and Tonto are able to expose the plot.

GUEST STARS: Chuck Courtney, House Peters Jr., Ken Duncan Jr., Kenneth MacDonald, Craig Duncan, Ted DeCorsia, Dick Wessell, Fred Libby, James Diehl

165) "Wanted: The Lone Ranger" (5/12/55)

When the Lone Ranger is framed for crimes by a vengeful gang, he has to clear his good name or find a price on his head.

GUEST STARS: Richard Travis, Sheb Wooley, Jesse White, Al Jackson, James Courtney, William Challey, Mike Dengate, Ray Saunders

166) "The Woman In The White Mask" (5/19/55)

When a young woman and her brother plan to resort to lawless means to seek vengeance, the Lone Ranger steps in to show them a better way.

GUEST STARS: Phyllis Coates, Jack Diamond, Chuck Courtney, Richard Reeves, Denver Pyle, Peter Thompson

167) "The Bounty Hunter" (5/26/55)

When bounty hunter Lex Sharp agrees to help the outlaw Glenn Bolton and hide him from the Lone Ranger, he's actually planning to turn the desperado in for the reward, and then break him out of jail again in a clever scheme where both crooks will come out ahead.

GUEST STARS: Russ Conway, Richard Reeves, Pierre Watkin, Gill Fallman

168) "Showdown At Sand Creek" (6/2/55)

James Houston steps in as sheriff when his older brother, Clay Houston, is killed. A friend of the family, the Lone Ranger has to prove to James that he's man enough to carry on his brother's work.

169) "Heart Of A Chester" (6/9/55)

The retired outlaw, Haskell, has regaled his grandson, Shelby, with tales of his past. But when Haskell agrees to hide two old pals, he has second thoughts when he sees how taken his grandson is with the life of an outlaw, and it's up to the Lone Ranger to prove that the path of honor is the better way.

GUEST STARS: Chuck Courtney, John Pickard, Tommy Ivo, Natalie Masters, Eddy Waller, William Challee

170) "The Swami" (6/16/55)

An old friend of the Lone Ranger's, Barnaby Boggs (see episodes 21 & 97), has been duped into being the front man for a crooked swami who hypnotizes people into revealing where they have gold hidden as he travels around the countryside in a wagon which houses a general store.

GUEST STARS: Hal Price, Chuck Courtney, Eddy Waller, Kem Dibbs, Earl Hodgins, Lou Krugman

171) "Sheriff For Sale" (6/23/55)

Hutch Conent runs the town of Nassaw, and when a new sheriff is appointed, Conent forges documents to make it appear the sheriff is crooked until the Lone Ranger and Tonto reveal who the real felon is.

GUEST STARS: Peter Hansen, Thurston Hall, Larry Blake

172) "Six-Gun Artist" (6/30/55)

Sheriff Will Harrington of Mesa Junction falls for a young woman who turns up in town claiming to be an artist. Only the Lone Ranger can prove that the young lady is the front-person for a gang of stage-robbers.

GUEST STARS: Guy Williams, Elaine Riley, Norman Willis, Mort Mills

173) "Death Goes To Press" (7/7/55)

Colonel Ingersoll is using his position as editor and publisher of the Daily Star to harm anyone who opposes his schemes until the Lone Ranger steps in.

GUEST STARS: Addison Richards, Kenneth MacDonald, Frank Ferguson, Guy Sorel, Peter Hansen

174) "Return Of Dice Dawson" (7/14/55)

Dice Dawson has reformed his outlaw ways and changed his name to Jay Thomasson. But when a series of crimes take place with a pair of black dice left at the scene (Dawson's old trademark), it takes the Lone Ranger to unravel the treacherous scheme.

GUEST STARS: Harry Carey Jr., Harry Lauter, Barbara Eiler, Herbert Heyes, Al Wyatt, James Todd

175) "Adventure At Arbuckle" (7/21/55)

Case Gordon has the town of Arbuckle in the palm of his hand, especially with his hired gun Dick Sundell as sheriff. Opposing him is Susan Starr, daughter of the town's recently murdered newspaper publisher. But she has someone else on her side—the Lone Ranger!

GUEST STARS: Nancy Leslie, William Challee, James Griffith, Lou Krugman, Paul Keats

176) "The Return" (7/28/55)

When Talana returns home to her tribe after being mission-educated for ten years, she finds that her brother is opposed to living in harmony with the settlers. When his renegade ways cause him to be captured by the Lone Ranger, her loyalty to her brother overcomes her better judgment and she helps the brave escape.

GUEST STARS: Yvette Dugay, Reed Howes, Terry Frost, Christopher Dark, Frank Wilcox

177) "Framed For Murder" (8/4/55)

When Tonto is framed for murder by the greedy, gold-crazed John Carter, the Lone Ranger must act fast to prove his old friend's innocence.

GUEST STARS: David Bruce, James Best, Whit Bissell, Jan Shepard, Robert Carson, Marshall Bradford

178) "Trapped" (8/11/55)

When Gaff Morgan and a youthful prisoner break out of jail, the Lone Ranger must find them and bring them back, and in the process tries to show the youth that the hard road chosen by Gaff Morgan is a grim and deadly path to follow.

GUEST STARS: John Doucette, Taggert Casey, Frank Ferguson, Robert Ellis, Marshall Bradford

179) "The Bait: Gold" (8/18/55)

When Terry Harding and his daughter fall plague to a series of robberies of gold shipments from their mine, they stand to lose everything when they can't meet their mortgage, until the Lone Ranger steps in.

GUEST STARS: Michael Whalen, Richard Avone, Hank Worden, Joan Hovis, George Neice, John Philips

180) "The Sheriff's Wife" (8/25/55)

When the Miles brothers terrorize the town of Parkersburg, they learn that the Lone Ranger and Tonto are after them and plot to ambush the masked man and his Indian companion.

GUEST STARS: John Bryant, Jack Elam, Joseph Turkel, Hugh Sandler, Elaine Edwards

181) "Counterfeit Redskins" (9/1/55)

The Lone Ranger and Tonto fight to prove that Indians aren't behind the vicious attacks on the homesteaders of Pine Valley, but that they're actually the work of outlaws bent on blaming the red man for their crimes.

GUEST STARS: Harry Lauter, Russell Johnson, Wayne Schaffer, Mel Welles, Paul Langton, Peter Mamakos, John Doucette

182) "One Nation Indivisible" (9/8/55)

The town of Mesa is still suffering from the days of the War Between The States, and it's up to the Lone Ranger to prove that the beliefs of Abraham Lincoln can help everyone.

GUEST STARS: Lyle Talbot, Roy Barcroft, Tyler McDuff, Watson Downs, Don Garner, Rand Brooks

SEASON FIVE (Episodes 183-221) all in color

183) "Wooden Rifle" (9/13/56)

Ed Decker is trying to gain control of all the land around Flat Rock. When Max Sunday stands in his way, he murders the man and frames Will Donoven for the crime.

GUEST STARS: Randy Brooks, Paul Engle, Bud Osborne, William Challee, Barbara Ann Kudson, Sidney Mason, Kay E. Kuter, Frank Scannell

184) "The Sheriff Of Smoke Tree" (9/20/56)

The Lem Crater gang is terrorizing the town of Smoke Tree until Buckley Webb arrives from Canyon City to assume the take over as the new sheriff. But the Lem Carter gang doesn't want another sheriff around to cramp their style.

GUEST STARS: Ron Haggerty, Slim Pickens, Tudor Owen, Claire Carlton, Mickey Simpson, John Bernadino, Lee Roberts

185) "Counterfeit Mask" (9/27/56)

When the Lone Ranger arrives in Silver Springs to visit his old friend there, who is sheriff, he's quickly arrested by his old friend for a string of murders and robberies. It seems that someone has been impersonating the Lone Ranger in order to destroy the masked man's good name, right down to using silver bullets in his crimes.

GUEST STARS: John Cliff, Paul Engle, Sandy Sanders, Sidney Mason, William Challee

186) "No Handicap" (10/4/56)

Sheriff Griff is blinded when shot by the Douglas gang during a bank robbery in Granite Creek. But the Lone Ranger proves that a blind man is not a useless man.

GUEST STARS: Will Wright, Ron Haggerty, Tudor Owen, Jim Parnell, Gary Marshall, John Bernadino, Mickey Simpson

187) "The Cross Of Santo Domingo" (10/11/56)

The cross of Santo Domingo is a rare and beautiful thing, and jeweler Arley McQueen wants to possess it for his own selfish motives.

GUEST STARS: Denver Pyle, Johnny Crawford, Jeanne Bates, Gregg Barton, Larry Johns, Lane Bradford, Rick Roman

188) "White Hawk's Decision" (10/18/56)

The son of Chief Imbray is slain by Drake, Slots and Willie Moon so that they can better steal the cattle on the Chief's land. Only the Lone Ranger can avert an all out war.

GUEST STARS: Robert Swan, Harry Lauter, Charles Stevens, Sandy Sanders, Ed Hashim, Louise Letterie, Holly Bane

189) "The Return Of Don Pedro O'Sullivan" (10/25/56)

Red-haired Don Pedro O'Sullivan, the fugitive revolutionary from Mexico, is returning to lead the revolt against the wicked General Sentore and Col. Ortega. When assassins attack Don Pedro and his daughter, the Lone Ranger and Tonto save them and come up with a clever plan to allow O'Sullivan to slip into Mexico by another route while the Ranger impersonates him. But when the plan is discovered, the Lone Ranger faces a firing squad.

GUEST STARS: George J. Lewis, John Bernadino, Tudor Owen, Maria Manay, Joe Vitale, Mickey Simpson

190) "Quicksand" (11/1/56)

When Mary Whitecloud is given gold by a rich cattleman to build a school for Indiana in Alkali Springs, greed overtakes Steve Grote and Blackhawk who kill the girl and flee with the gold. But can the Lone Ranger be far behind?

GUEST STARS: William Henry, Terry Frost, Denver Pyle, Henry Rowland, Robert Burton, Rick Roman

191) "Quarterhorse War" (11/8/56)

Sheriff Ed McGuire is still bitter that he lost a girl to Mark Allen. To get back at him he steals the prize money for a horse race and frames Mark for the crime.

GUEST STARS: Harry Lauter, William Tannen, Mae Morgan, Charles Stevens, George Mather, Holly Bane

192) "The Letter Bride" (11/15/56)

Some of the people of Forgens Flat don't want Chinese people moving in. To force out Lee Po they kidnap his girlfriend, but the Lone Ranger considers racism a particularly ugly crime.

GUEST STARS: Victor Sen Young, Slim Pickens, Dennis Moore, John Bernadino, John Vital, Ray Jones, Lee Roberts, Judy Dan, Mickey Simpson, Claire Carlton, Tudor Owen

193) "Hot Spell In Panamint" (11/22/56)

If Roy Bell, the marshall of Panamint, won't release the outlaw known as the Sonora Kid from jail, Big Joe Hunsinger plans to shoot the lawman down.

GUEST STARS: Ran Brooks, Sandy Sanders, Don C. Harvey, Barbara Ann Kudson, Sidney Mason, William Challee, Wally West, Rudy Bowman, John Cliff

194) "The Twisted Track" (11/29/56)

Wynn and Clint Harkey believe that Frank Miller is responsible for

Clint's war wound, so they come to Miller Junction to settle up with the man once and for all.

GUEST STARS: William Henry, Greg Barton, Terry Frost, Tyler McDuff, Robert Burton, Frank Hagney

195) "Decision For Chris McKeever" (12/6/56)

The McKeever gang is determined to get revenge for the death of their parents at the hands of lawmen. Their first step is to steal the gold shipment from a stagecoach.
GUEST STARS: George Mather, William Tannen, Robert Swan, Sandy Sanders

196) "Trouble At Tylerville" (12/13/56)

The people of Tylerville aren't too happy about having ex-con Roy Hillman coming there to live after the man's father dies and leaves his son his home. The Lone Ranger proves that everyone deserves a second chance once they've paid their debt to society.
GUEST STARS: Tom Brown, Ben Weldon, Mary Ellen Kaye, John Pickard, Francis MacDonald, Charles Aldridge

197) "Christmas Story" (12/20/56)

When Ben Talbot's common sense is overwhelmed by the chance for quick riches, he deserts his family to try to make a gold strike. But they are reunited when he returns home Christmas day a wiser man.
GUEST STARS: Bill Henry, Jimm Baird, Mary Newton, Aline Towne, Gregg Barton, Robert Burton, Lane Bradford, Terry Frost

198) "Ghost Canyon" (12/27/56)

When two men discover silver in Buffalo Canyon, they try to get Fleet Horse to kill his brother Little Hawk who would stop them from getting the silver for themselves.
GUEST STARS: Ed Hashim, Robert Swan, Harry Lauter, Holly Bane, Charles Stevens

199) "Outlaw Masquerade" (1/3/57)

The ghost town of Rim Rock is the destination of three desperadoes who break out of prison to retrieve the one million dollars in gold they hid there.
GUEST STARS: Richard Crane, Joseph Crehan, House Peters Jr., Steve Rich

200) "The Avenger" (1/10/57)

When Mark Rote sees his father gunned down and is then forced to shoot his father's killer to protect himself, he's given the job of sheriff of Cottonwood. But Mark is overzealous in his pursuit of crime and almost slays an innocent man until the Lone Ranger shows him the real meaning of justice.
GUEST STARS: Tris Coffin, Richard Benedict, Roy Barcroft, Alan Wells, Francis MacDonald, Dennis Moore, Kay E. Kuter

201) "The Courage Of Tonto" (1/17/57)

Sgt. Red Cloud blames the Lone Ranger for leading his father to the site where he was ambushed by Lou Pierson, who shot Chief Gray Horse in the back.
GUEST STARS: Maurice Jara, Joe Ashley, Francis MacDonald, Edwin Mitchell, Jim Bannon

202) "The Breaking Point" (1/24/57)

After gold is found in Eagle

Pass, the Slade gang goes on a claim-jumping spree, murdering anyone who opposes them.

GUEST STARS: Richard Crane, Ken Dibbs, Brad Morrow, Keith Richards, Charles Weggenheim, House Peters Jr.

203) "A Harp For Hannah" (1/31/57)

When Walter Dubbs saves up money to buy his wife a harp, Wes Talman, the son of a wealthy ranch owner, cheats Walter out of his hard earned cash.

GUEST STARS: Pierce Leyden, Trevor Bardette, Bob Roarke, John Cason, Louise Lewis, Ralph Sanford

204) "A Message From Abe" (2/7/57)

When the wife of ex-con Phil Beach is in desperate need of medical attention, he robs her father of his life savings in hopes of saving the woman's life.

GUEST STARS: James Griffith, Harry Strang, Don C. Harvey, Mauritz Hugo, Maggie O'Bryne

205) "Code Of Honor" (2/14/57)

Three outlaws disguise themselves as soldiers in order to rob gold from prospectors on their way to the bank. But their scheme has other wrinkles and so they kidnap Captain Davis near Fort Brady to complete their treacherous plan.

GUEST STARS: Paul Engle, William Callee, Randy Brooks, Helen Marshall, Kay E. Kuter, John Cliff, Sandy Sanders, John Maxwell, Don. C. Harvey

206) "The Turning Point" (2/21/57)

When crime seems out of control in Blue River, a man named Bennett leads a band of vigilantes to make their own law. But only the Lone Ranger can do that!

GUEST STARS: Paul Campbell, Pierce Leyden, George Barrows, Margaret Syewart, John Cason

207) "Dead Eye" (2/28/57)

Dallas "Dead Eye" Jones and the Lone Ranger team up in Silver City to bring the desperadoes Tanner and Beaudry to justice.

GUEST STARS: Don Murray, William Fawcett, Nolan Leary, Myron Healey

208) "Clover In The Dust" (3/7/57)

Will Yeomans, son of rancher Jeff Yeomans, is killed in cold blood when he catches Matt Thorne, his father's foreman, rustling cattle. Only the Lone Ranger can ease the rancher's grief by bringing the killer to justice.

GUEST STARS: Dan Barton, Harry Strange, Syd Mason, Don C. Harvey

209) "Slim's Boy" (3/14/57)

Gil Ryan has been released from prison after eight years and is riding back to get his revenge on the man who put him there, sheriff Sam Masters. But crippling arthritis has robbed Masters of his once fast draw and Ryan is also planning to lure into crime the young man Masters helped raise unless the Lone Ranger can help justice to win out.

GUEST STARS: Bob Roarke, Trevor Bardett, John Cason, Pierce Leyden, Louise Lewis

210) "Two Against Two" (3/21/57)

Vic Foley double-crosses his partner Eduardo Mendosa after they grab a thousand dollars in a bank robbery by shooting him in the back. But the Lone Ranger learns the truth when he finds Mendoas and they have a showdown in Devil's Canyon.

GUEST STARS: Baynes Barrow, Garry Murray, Eugenia Paul

211) "Ghost Town Fury" (3/28/57)

The Clanton brothers return to their old robbing ways when they break out of prison and start holding up stage coaches out in the Badlands until the Lone Ranger happens along.

GUEST STARS: Richard Crane, Carlos Vera, House Peters Jr., Steve Rich, Kem Dibbs

212) "The Prince Of Buffalo Gap" (4/4/57)

When young Prince Maximillian visits Buffalo Gap, his uncle hires outlaw Matt Cagle to kill the prince and make it look like a buffalo hunting accident. But when the prince overhears his uncle plotting, he flees and encounters the Lone Ranger, who concocts a counterplot with the prince.

GUEST STARS: Robert Crossman, Gabor Curtis, Michael Winkleman, Jim Bannon

213) "The Law And Miss Aggie" (4/11/57)

Years ago the Apaches killed Aggie Turner's husband and kidnapped her young son. When the Lone Ranger discovers that the boy has been raised by the Apaches, he has to prove to Aggie that her son is still alive and overcome her bitterness against Indians.

GUEST STARS: Florence Lake, Dennis Moore, Buddy Baer, John Vital, Brad Johnson

214) "The Tarnished Star" (4/18/57)

When the Lone Ranger comes to Peaceful Valley to visit an old friend, he learns that the man was killed years before and his wife has remarried. Her new husband is sheriff, and some suspect that he's deliberately allowing the notorious False Face gang to rob unchecked. When the Lone Ranger uncovers the truth, a man has to decide to do what is right, no matter what it costs him.

GUEST STARS: Paul Engle, Myron Healey, Don Murray, William Fawcett, Mercedes Shirley, Rudy Bowman

215) "Canuck" (4/25/57)

When Canadians start settling in Vandalia, Dan Slussen sells them cattle with bills of sale written in disappearing ink, and then has his men accuse the Canucks of cattle rustling and shoot them down. When a wealthy Canuck on his way to Vandalia is slain, the Lone Ranger temporarily disguises himself as the man to get to the truth and expose the killers.

GUEST STARS: Tris Coffin, Roy Barcroft, Virginia Christine, Richard Benedict, Peter Miles, Kay E. Kuter

216) "Mission For Tonto" (5/2/57)

When Tonto and the Lone Ranger find a wounded man floating down the river, they uncover the scheme of a woman and her ex-con sons to murder a rancher's grandson so that they can take the ranch for themselves after their mother marries the rancher. When Tonto unwittingly leads the murderers back to the wounded man, he learns the truth in time to smash the plot.

GUEST STARS: Florence Lake, Robert Burton, Lane Bradford, Gregg Barton, Tyler McDuff

217) "Journey To San Carlos" (5/9/57)

When Chief Blue Feather's brother breaks the treaty and rides off with a band of renegades to attack the settlers, the Lone Ranger pleads with the Chief to help them stop the killing. When a guide who fled from a previous Indian attack (at the cost of his whole party) tries to regain his nerve by hitting the trail again with a brother and sister going to San Carlos, everything comes to a head when the renegade Piutes attack.

GUEST STARS: Myron Healey, Rick Vallin, Joe Sargeant, Melinda Byron, Harry Strang

218) "The Banker's Son" (5/16/57)

When the son of the Two Rivers bank president accidentally shoots his father, he panics when he realizes that Tonto was a witness and runs to the sheriff to blame Tonto, hoping sheriff Hendrick will kill the Indian before the truth comes out.

GUEST STARS: Jim Bannon, Edwin Mitchell, Hank Worden, Ron Haggerty

219) "The Angel And The Outlaw" (5/23/57)

When the Cattlemen's Association in Denton is robbed by the Calico Kid and his gang, the Lone Ranger and Tonto move in to bring the outlaws to justice.

GUEST STARS: Florence Lake, Linda Wrather, Dennis Moore, Brad Johnson, Carlos Vera

220) "Blind Witness" (5/30/57)

The express office in Flat Rock is robbed by the Grody Brothers, thanks to inside information provided by Benson, the town's watchmaker, who's secretly part of the notorious outlaw gang. But there was an unlikely witness to the crime.

GUEST STARS: William Fawcett, Nolan Leary, Myron Healey, Don Murray, Kay Riehl, Byron Foulger

221) "Outlaws In Greasepaint" (6/6/57)

The traveling acting troupe of Lavina and Dewitt Faversham actually are using the their roles as cover for the robberies they commit behind the scenes at the Wells Fargo offices. But in Cedar Springs they encounter the Lone Ranger and Tonto backstage and the curtain is brought down on the thespian thieves.

GUEST STARS: Tom Brown, John Pickard, Ben Welden

Repeats aired on network until 1961 but no new TV episodes were made in this series after the '56-'57 season.

The 39 color episodes were a creative decision made by Jack Wrather after he acquired the rights to the Lone Ranger in 1954. These color episodes were re-edited into 13 features for TV syndication which each contain three episodes, and are sometimes packaged as a series under the overall title "Justice Of The West." Each one is called THE ADVENTURES OF THE LONE RANGER and each has a separate secondary title at the end of the introductory section. The introductory section is the same for each of the 13 feature compilations and consists of the origin of the Lone Ranger which was originally presented at the opening of the 1958 feature THE LONE RANGER AND THE LOST CITY OF GOLD. As the origin segment begins, the main title

THE ADVENTURES OF THE LONE RANGER flashes on the screen in yellow letters, and at the conclusion of the origin the separate compilation title flashes on the screen in white letters. All episodes are shown complete except that two out of the three have the final scene in which the Ranger calls out "Hi-Yo Silver, Away!" rather sloppily cut out so that someone will say, "Why, he's the Lone Ranger!" and the scene suddenly jumps into the beginning of the next adventure. Even though the final episode has the final scene on it, even that is jumpy as though all the final scenes were cut out and then one was tacked on later rather than just leaving one of the three episodes intact to start with. Prints currently in syndication look like old 16mm prints rather than new prints transferred from the original negatives to videotape as they tend to appear faded, dirty and scratched. Each runs 77 minutes.

The thirteen compilations break down into individual episodes as follows.

THE ADVENTURES OF THE LONE RANGER (compilations)

1) CHAMPIONS OF JUSTICE
"Blind Witness" (#220)
"Clover In The Dust" (#208)
"The Angle And The Outlaw" (#219)

2) COUNT THE CLUES
"Wooden Rifle" (#183)
"The Sheriff Of Smoke Tree" (#184)
"Ghost Town Fury" (#211)

3) JUSTICE OF THE WEST
"Outlaw Masquerade" (#199)
"Quicksand" (#190)
"No Handicap" (#186)

4) THE LAWLESS
"Slim's Boy" (#209)
"The Return Of Don Pedro O'Sullivan" (#189)
"The Tarnished Star" (#214)

5) MASQUERADE
"The Turning Point" (#206)
"Code Of Honor" (#205)
"Dead Eye" (#207)

6) MORE THAN MAGIC
"Outlaws In Greasepaint" (#221)
"White Hawk's Decision" (#188)
"Hot Spell In Panamint" (#193)

7) NOT ABOVE SUSPICION
"The Avenger" (#200)
"Mission For Tonto" (#216)
"Journey To San Carlos" (#217)

8) ONE MASK TOO MANY
"The Prince Of Buffalo Gap" (#212)
"Canuck" (#215)
"Counterfeit Mask" (#185)

9) THE SEARCH
"Christmas Story" (#197)
"The Cross Of Santo Domingo" (#187)
"The Breaking Point" (#202)

10) TALE OF GOLD
"Quarterhorse War" (#191)
"A Harp For Hannah" (#203)
"Decision For Chris McKeever"

11) THE TRACKERS
"The Twisted Track" (#194)
"Trouble At Tylerville" (#196)
"Ghost Canyon" (#198)

12) THE TRUTH
"The Banker's Son" (#218)
"The Letter Bride" (#192)
"The Law And Miss Aggie" (#213)

13) VENGEANCE VOW
"Two Against Two" (#210)
"A Message From Abe" (#204)
"The Courage Of Tonto" (#201)

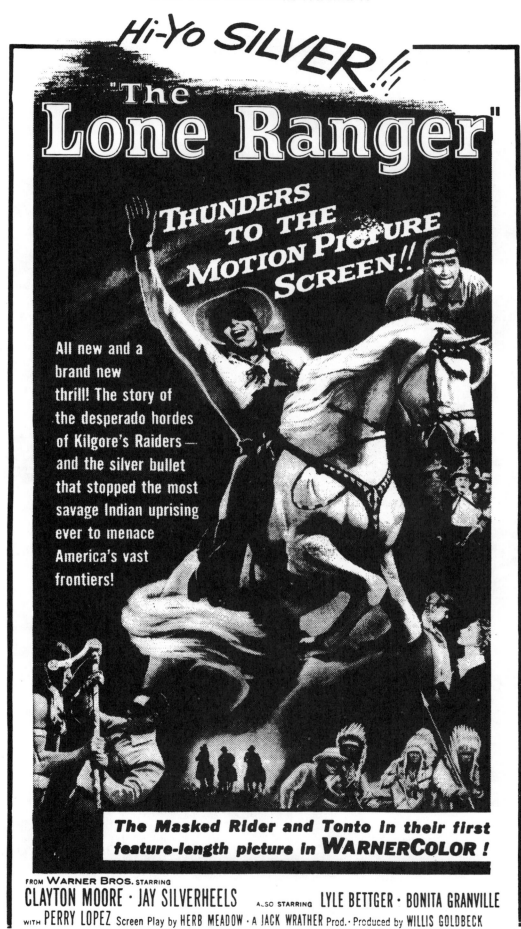

The Lone Ranger At the Movies

During the mid-Fifties, the Lone Ranger came thundering across the screen in two color spectacles: THE LONE RANGER (1956) and THE LONE RANGER AND THE LOST CITY OF GOLD (1957). Clayton Moore and Jay Silverheels continued the roles with which their names had become synonymous to television audiences.

The first of these two features was made by Warner Brothers while the second was released by United Artists, although both were Jack Wrather Productions. Wrather had acquired the Lone Ranger property from George W. Trendle and he maintained it until his death.

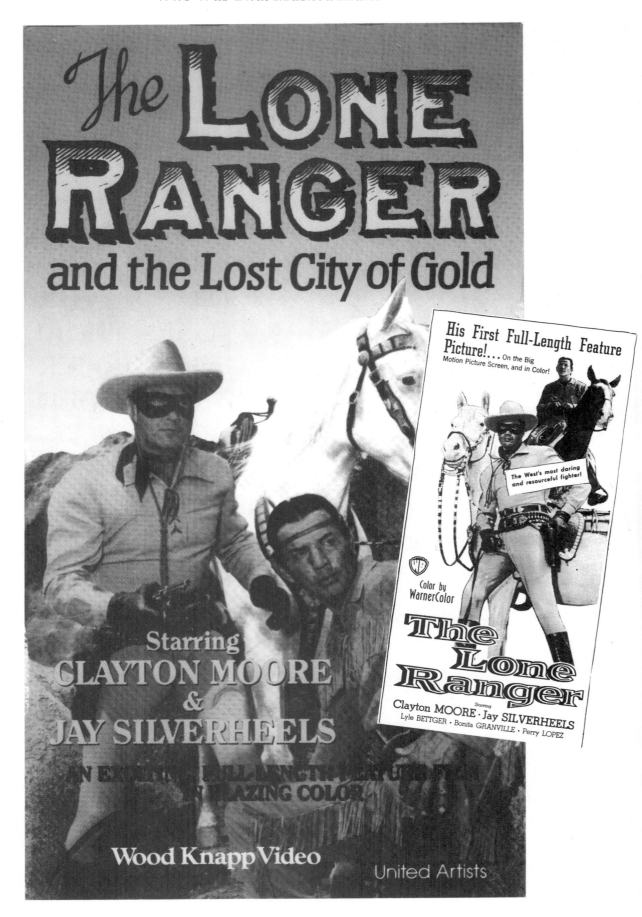

The Lone Ranger
(1956)

Credits
The Lone Ranger: Clayton Moore
Tonto: Jay Silverheels
Reece Kilgore: Lyle Bettger
Welcome Kilgore:
                    Bonita Granville
Ramirez: Perry Lopez
Cassidy: Robert Wilke
Sheriff Kimberly: John Pickard
Angry Horse: Michael Ansara
The Governor: Charles Meredith
Lila Kilgore: Beverly Washburn
Red Hawk: Frank deKova
Powder: Mickey Simpson
Goss: Zon Murry
Whitebeard: Lane Chandler
The Old Prospector:
                    Clayton Moore

Director: Stuart Heisler
Screenplay: Herb Meadow
Cinematography:
                    Edwin DuPar, A.S.C.
Filmed in WarnerColor
Produced by Willis Goldbech
Art Director: Stanley Fleischer
Musical Score: David Buttolph
Film Editor:
                    Clarence Kolster, A.C.E.
Sound by M.A. Merrich
Set Decorator: G.W. Bernsten
Makeup Supervisor:
                    Gordon Bau, S.M.A.
Assistant Director: Robert Farfan

A Jack Wrather Production
Released through Warner Brothers

Running Time: 86 minutes

This film opens with a spectacular panorama of the masked man and Tonto observing an Indian attack in a valley far below, whereupon they ride down to the victim's aid. Directed by Stuart Heisler, the film has the sense of scope and spectacle which one expects from a theatrical production. The story, although using the Western cliche of a rancher employing white men disguised as Indians to cause trouble, is handled well and is bolstered by a good script and fine acting. The film has a genuine sense of style and drama and isn't just a padded TV script.

The pacing of THE LONE RANGER is flawless and includes excellent fight scenes as well as a number of fantastic stunts. One such stunt, the best in the picture, in fact, occurs when you least expect it. The main villain of the story has just been killed and the principal henchman, Cassidy, is fleeing from the Ranger across an expansive plain. Their horses proceed down a steep incline whereupon the Ranger leaps from Silver down onto Cassidy, ripping the thug from his saddle while both hit the ground and take a tremendous rolling fall down the hill—and believe me, it's steep! It's a particularly fast and furious segment. At the conclusion of their fight at the bottom of the hill, the slope appears in the background and it's clear that it is quite steep and wasn't just accomplished through trick photography. The location shooting in the rangeland of southern Utah is spectacular. A number of panoramic shots in the film, particularly the one at the open, are awe inspiring and add considerably to the flavor of the film.

THE LONE RANGER is the best of the two films as it possesses thrills the second picture just didn't succeed in attaining.

The Lone Ranger And The Lost City Of Gold
(1958)

Credits
The Lone Ranger: Clayton Moore
Tonto: Jay Silverheels
Ross Brady: Douglas Kennedy
Oscar Matthison: Charles Watts
Frances Henderson: Noreen Nash
Paviva: Lisa Montell
Padre Vicente Esteban:
                            Ralph Moody
Dr. James Rolfe: Norman Frederic
Tomache: John Miljan
Redbird: Maurice Jara
Travers: Bill Henry
Wilson: Lane Bradford
Caulama Belle Mitchell

Director: Lesley Selander
Producer: Sherman A. Harris
Screenplay:
 Robert Schaefer & Eric Freiwald
Music: Les Baxter
Song "Hi Yo Silver" by Lenny
Adelson and Les Baxter
Director of Photography:
            Kenneth Peach, A.S.C.
Film Editor:
            Robert S. Golden, A.S.E.

A Jack Wrather Production
Released through United Artists

Running Time: 80 minutes

In comparison with the first film, THE LONE RANGER AND THE LOST CITY OF GOLD is found wanting. While not a bad film, it is essentially just a puffed up TV episode, although it does include nice moments. The best sequence is the pre-title segment which recounts the origin of THE LONE RANGER visually beneath a song which explains what is shown. Those few minutes possess a charm which bears viewing over and over again. All though the brief recap of the origin, a song titled "Hi-Yo Silver" plays, adding mood to the recap. It was considered to be so effective that when the 39 half-hour color episodes of the TV series were cut into 13 seventy-seven minute features for TV syndication, that origin sequence was cut into the open of each film so the Lone Ranger would be quickly introduced and set up for viewers since. The TV episodes assume those watching already know the legend of the Lone Ranger.

Although once again filmed on location, the photography lacks inspiration, primarily due to the director, Lesley Selander.

A prevalent theme in both Lone Ranger films quite beneficial to the pictures, is racism against Indians. Both films slam bigotry leaving no question in the mind of the viewer that this film has something to say on the subject. In THE LOST CITY OF GOLD this presents itself in the form of a doctor, played by Norman Frederic, passing for white, although he's really an Indian. He uses his respected position in the town to try to control the often shabby treatment Indians receive from the townspeople, particularly the sheriff. In THE LONE RANGER Indians are also treated as second class citizens by many whites climaxing in Tonto barely escaping hanging at the hands of an angry mob. Jay Silverheels always made it evident by his actions that he never felt inferior. He takes on a ruthless gang, battling them in a long fist-fight sequence before be-

ing overwhelmed by sheer numbers.

In CITY OF GOLD, Tonto stands up to the bigoted sheriff when he threatens an Indian girl, and gets shot down for his trouble by the cowardly lawman. Because it happens in the middle of town, and the doctor chooses that moment to reveal his Indian heritage, the ugliness of racism is made even more evident. At the end of the scene, when the townspeople turn their backs on the sheriff and walk away, it is quite effective.

While both THE LONE RANGER and THE LONE RANGER AND THE LOST CITY OF GOLD are good films, the first one holds up better under repeated viewing, the true test of an effective film.

The Legend Of The Lone Ranger
(1981)

Credits
The Lone Ranger:
Klinton Spilsbury
Tonto: Michael Horse
Cavendish: Christopher Lloyd
Sheriff Wiatt: Matt Clark
Amy Striker: Juanin Clay
President Grant: Jason Robards
Dan Reid: John Bennett Perry
Collins: David Hayward
Lucas Striker: John Hart
Wild Bill Hickok:
Richard Farnsworth
General Custer: Lincoln Tate
Buffalo Bill Cody: Ted Flicker
Young John Reid: Marc Gilpin
Young Tonto: Patrick Montoya
General Rodriguez: David Bennett
German Passenger: Rick Traeger

The Gambler: James Bowman
Chinese Passenger: Kit Wong
Waystation Agent: Daniel Nunez
Stagecoach Driver: R.L. Tolbert
Shotgun: Clay Boss
First Chief: Jose Rey Toledo
Second Chief: Max Cisneros
Mr. Reid: Ted White
Mrs. Reid: Chere Bryson
Waiter: James Lee Crite

Director: William A. Fraker
Screenplay:
Ivan Goff & Ben Roberts
andMichael Kane
and William Roberts
Adaptation: Jerry Derloshon
Executive Producer:
Martin Starger
Director of Photography:
Laszlo Kovacs, A.S.C.
Production Designer:
Albert Brenner
Edited by
Thomas Stanford, A.C.E.
The Story of "The Man In The Mask"
sung by Merle Haggard
Lyrics: Dean Pitchford
Original Music: John Barry
Costume Designer: Noel Taylor
Additional Photography:
Bobby Byrne
Sound Mixer: William Randall
Supervising Sound Editor:
Gordon Ecker, Jr.
Music Editor:
Clifford C. Kohlweck

Filmed on location in New Mexico, Utah and Nevada

Running Time: 98 minutes

THE LEGEND OF THE LONE RANGER was shrouded in controversy almost from the beginning. As soon as this first theatrical version of the character in over twenty years was announced, the Wrather Corporation (then the owners of all rights to the Lone Ranger, and Clayton Moore's former employer) took legal action to prevent Moore from appearing in public in a mask or identifying himself as the Lone Ranger. Jack Wrather's company was apparently afraid the general public wouldn't understand that the man who played the Lone Ranger last in 1958 was not the same man who was to appear as the Lone Ranger in the 1981 feature film. When the dust settled, Moore was reduced to wearing wraparound sunglasses and was so embittered by the experience that when the producers of the film attempted to make it up to him by giving him a role in the movie, he flatly turned them down. That wasn't the only controversy.

On March 27, 1980, a press event to introduce the new Lone Ranger and Tonto was held on Hollywood Boulevard, where the previous summer Jay Silverheels had been honored with a star on the renowned Walk of Fame. Klinton Spilsbury and Michael Horse rode up to Mann's Chinese Theatre on horseback where the event was to take place. Trouble brewed when the two performers appeared for only a few minutes, refused to talk to anyone, and were then hustled off! The TV crews did get some footage, but the printed press were left empty-handed. They had been understandably curious about the new Lone Ranger and how he sounded; afterwards they cracked jokes that Spilsbury's voice was so awful Clayton Moore would dub it in the film. An amusing idea and closer to the truth than any imagined at the time.

On February 27, 1981, THE LEGEND OF THE LONE RANGER had a sneak preview in San Diego which bore an intro explaining that it was a "work in progress" to be further refined before regular release. That version seemed quite complete and no differences were visible when it was released officially on May 22nd.

While the film remains true to the Lone Ranger's origin as previously portrayed, this time the story begins much earlier than the canyon ambush of the Texas Rangers. The film opens with John Reid as a boy hiding a young Tonto from marauding outlaws, only to see those same outlaws murder his own parents. Tonto then takes young John to his village where he lives for a short time, learning the things other young warriors learn, until his older brother, Dan, sends him back east.

Years later, John Reid returns to Texas as a lawyer bent on helping his brother. This leads into the massacre of the Texas Rangers and Tonto once more finding his blood brother whom he recognizes by a medallion given young John years before. The two men having first met as boys was portrayed previously in the first episode of the LONE RANGER TV series in 1949, but the film expands on this incident.

Unlike in earlier versions of this story, Tonto expresses contempt for the way whites have treated the Indian and refuses to be bound to a reservation. He searches for justice for his people just as John Reid seeks justice for the murder of his brother and the other Texas Rangers. In fact, near the end of the film when President Grant asks Tonto if there's any way he can repay him for his help, Tonto asks the President to honor the treaties which the U.S. has signed with his brothers. Grant replies that he'll try, and the bitter irony is not lost on anyone in the audience.

THE LEGEND OF THE LONE RANGER seemed to have a hopeful future. Michael Horse captured a sense of individuality and pride that made him much more than just the Lone Ranger's faithful Indian companion. In this film, he becomes the Lone Ranger's equal. Only in the two feature films released in '56 and '58 was the part of Tonto expanded enough for Jay Silverheels to be more than just a sidekick.

Klinton Spilsbury looked much better on screen than in publicity photos, although the producers apparently weren't completely satisfied as they found it necessary to have actor James Keach re-dub his voice. Unless you knew that ahead of time, you'd have no reason to notice as the dubbing is done very skillfully. This and other considerations made it tough sledding for Spilsbury when the film was released. Like Sam Jones who played Flash Gordon, Spilsbury had skeletons in his closet which the press quickly unearthed. He apparently had an antagonistic attitude towards doing publicity for the film. For the New Year's parade held on January 1, 1981, the Lone Ranger and Tonto appear, but a substitute rode in Spilsbury's saddle while Michael Horse appeared as Tonto. Unsavory stories of Spilsbury's performance off-screen filtered out, including a tale of him slapping a waitress across the face and being barred from two watering holes in Santa Fe for fighting when the film was on location. When Jim Steranko questioned director William Fraker about these reports in MEDIASCENE/PREVUE #43, Fraker did not deny them. Even when the film was released, there were no interviews with Spilsbury. Months later he appeared in a small segment on a syndicated series about TV Westerns which looked as if it may have been filmed while the movie was on location. That interview put to rest rumors that there was anything wrong with the actor's voice. It was fine. It may well have been that his voice was dubbed because all films have lines looped (re-recorded) in post-production, and James Keach may have been brought in because Spilsbury was uncooperative. A similar situation occurred in the movie POPEYE when an actor's voice was completely re-dubbed because he'd proved difficult to work with on set.

Director William Fraker brought a lot of style to this modern big-screen translation of the legend. He clearly attempts to emulate John Ford, even going so far as shooting on some of the same desert terrain Ford used in the 1939 classic STAGECOACH.

There were reports the film suffered location problems from snow when a scene suddenly includes large patches of snow in the background which appear nowhere else in the movie. Considering that many scenes involve desert and near-desert conditions, the snow is jarring.

At only just over an hour and a half, the film ends very quickly because more than half of the time is spent on the Lone Ranger's origin. With the average big-budget film normally running close to two hours, it's not unreasonable to have expected this one to be a little longer, especially when so much time had to be spent setting up the story. The film also suffers from the basic problem of much of the story being familiar. Although additional characterization helps make the film more interesting, character interplay ceases once the

Ranger dons his mask. Tonto then slips once more into the background while the Lone Ranger develops a studied cold gaze apparently designed to make him look serious in an outlandish outfit for a Western setting. Still, there is a genuine thrill when John Reid stands over his brother's grave and vows justice and then turns around to face the camera wearing the mask for the first time. This dissolves into almost ethereal slow-motion footage of the Ranger and Tonto riding through the desert.

As interesting as the film is, with such touches as Jason Robards as U.S. Grant and a salute to stunt great Yakima Canutt in the form of a variation on his famous under-the-stagecoach bit, the film is really only a sixteen million dollar television episode. It's entertaining and fun, but fails to grasp the scope of a theatrical feature.

The film suffered script problems as evidenced when the director stated there were two different scripts when he came on the project and the screen credits list four writers on the screenplay plus an "adaptation by" credit. They tried hard to make that transfer once again from radio and small screen to the big screen, but inhibited by the long origin, they wrapped up the Butch Cavendish story too quickly. The film falls short of its goal. The 1956 film managed the transition far better with only one screenwriter. Yet even if THE LEGEND OF THE LONE RANGER isn't a great film, it is a good one. With the emotional Clayton Moore controversy long behind us, perhaps it can now be viewed more fairly.

It still stands as the last Lone Ranger tale although rumors have surfaced recently about plans to try another big screen feature for release in 1991, a decade after the last attempt. Whether that turns out to be more than just speculation remains to be seen at writing.

SPECIAL SECTION

John Hart Forgotten Ranger

Born December 13, 1917, John Hart began his acting career in the Thirties in THE BUCCANEER (1937) and appeared in other films such as DISBARRED, UNION PACIFIC, HUNTED MEN and MILLION DOLLAR LEGS. After serving in World War Two, Hart starred in the serial JACK ARMSTRONG in 1947. In the Fifties, he worked extensively on television and played the Lone Ranger in 52 episodes of the series. He starred with Lon Chaney Jr. in the syndicated series HAWKEYE AND THE LAST OF THE MOHICANS and appeared in numerous other TV episodes such as SKY KING, RAWHIDE, RIN-TIN-TIN, SGT. PRESTON, FURY, and others. He also starred in the Columbia serial THE ADVENTURES OF CAPTAIN AFRICA. In the Eighties, Hart appeared in a supporting role in THE LEGEND OF THE LONE RANGER (1981) and played the Lone Ranger in one episode each of HAPPY DAYS and THE GREATEST AMERICAN HERO. Today he is retired and lives in Warner Springs, California.

John Hart, the television Lone Ranger from 1952 until 1954, makes a special appearance in costume for the HAPPY DAYS series. Here he meets the Fonz, one of the Ranger's greatest fans.

HOW DID YOU BECOME IN- VOLVED IN FILMS?

I actually grew up in San Ma- rino, which is near Pasadena, and my mother was a drama critic on the local paper. She became very well-known as a drama critic and this was in the Thirties when the Pasadena Playhouse was really a major theatre. Outside of New York it was probably the number one community theatre. She cov- ered all the shows at the playhouse for years and I started going to see plays when I was in high school and even before that. So I got re- ally close to the theatre at an early age and thought it was just great.

Bill Holden (his real name was Billy Beadle) and I went to South Pasadena High School together and we both decided we'd try to be actors. So we took drama in school and then I did quite a few shows at the Pasadena Playhouse. A friend of mine got me into a big agency, the Myron Selznick Agen- cy, which was one of the biggies of the time, and I got a job on a (Cecil B.) DeMille picture. Every- body liked me so I got a contract at Paramount and worked on a bunch of pictures. This was in '37 to '39.

WHAT WAS THE FIRST FILM YOU APPEARED IN?

That was THE BUCCANEER (1938) which was a C.B. DeMille big-budget feature. I think it was one of the first pictures that An- thony Quinn ever appeared in. It starred Fredric March and a very pretty Austrian leading lady named Franciska Gaal. Akim Ta- miroff was in it. DeMille always used first class people, and all the good character people. I got to know Fredric March a little bit— he was a very interesting man.

Then I worked in a bunch more DeMille pictures through the years.

WHAT WAS DeMILLE LIKE?

He was a very interesting guy. He was an absolute gentleman most of the time. Very business- like and he could handle big sets, with 400 people, 50 chickens, 20 cows; he had a very marvelous tal- ent for doing things like that. He demanded complete attention when he was working because his pictures were quite expensive, and about once every two weeks on a show, he'd just blow up and start screaming and yelling at every- body. And he'd pick out some poor assistant director or maybe some bit player who wasn't pay- ing attention. When he flipped one of these fits it was embarrassing and everybody just cringed. When he got through with it then every- body paid attention!

But I'd been to his house and he always knew me by name and lat- er in the years, being an out-of- work actor, if he had something going, I could always go do so- mething in it. I liked him and he liked me. He had a certain kind of people that he really liked and he was very loyal to them. Almost the same group worked in all his pictures.

They say he slept only four or five hours a night and was a wor- kaholic. He had a nice wife and a lovely home in the Los Feliz area and he was a charming gentleman when things were under control. A very brilliant man.

WHAT FILMS DID YOU GO INTO AFTER WORKING ON THE DeMILLE FILMS?

This was the late Thirties, the days of the big studios way before television. Studios turned out a certain number of features and

they had "A" pictures, which were your big-budget and a whole cult of "B" pictures with a much lower budget and a faster shooting schedule. The "B" pictures had their "B" stars who were wonderful people and it was like a little stock company. I don't know how many I worked in with people like Lloyd Nolan, Bob Preston, Tony Quinn, Mary Carlisle, and they were stars of their day. The studios were on a gangster kick in those days. KING OF ALCATRAZ (1938) was one of them. But I worked in fifteen or twenty features during that time.

DID YOU MAINTAIN CONTACT WITH WILLIAM HOLDEN?

No, not really. He was a very strange guy. I got a contract with Paramount before he did and then he came, and they had a little stock contract. I met him at the studio and said, "Hey, Bill, let me show you around and introduce you to anybody." We did a little bit of that and then about two weeks later I picked up the paper and he'd landed the lead in GOLDEN BOY opposite Barbara Stanwyck at Columbia. So Paramount made some deal with him at Columbia, and although we'd been friends for years, I hardly ever saw him again. I'd run into him once in awhile.

In the picture business, as in most any other businesses, you help your friends. You work for a director and he likes you, you do a good job, and someone will say so-and-so is making a picture and you run over and get a job—that's the way you stay alive. You help each other. Bill became a big star very fast and I became a freelance actor after a year and a half at Paramount, and so I was out there hustling jobs. It was feast or famine. When you worked it was marvelous. When you didn't it was terrible. But the few times I ran into Bill, he'd never say, "Hey, we're starting something over at Fox," or that I should go see somebody. He never did a thing to help me. He was kind of an alcoholic in high school, too, and that was a very sad way that he passed away. But he was an interesting guy, too.

WHAT WAS IT LIKE WORKING WITH LON CHANEY, JR?

That was on a TV series called HAWKEYE AND THE LAST OF THE MOHICANS and Chaney was my faithful Indian companion, Chingachgook. Just like I did on THE LONE RANGER, I had a faithful Indian companion and Lon was another strange guy. We made the series in Canada, out of Toronto, on a financing arrangement called the "E Plan" where a large portion of the crew below the director or assistant director had to be Canadian or English. There were a lot of advantages to it and it was really an excellent program, but I guess not many people could figure it out so it wasn't used too much.

Chaney and I moved up to Toronto for almost a year making the show. He used to drink. I guess everybody knows that. He died from drinking too damn much. But he was a consummate actor. Boy he was good. He knew every trick. It was an education working with him, and we were always good friends. I never had any problems with him. But you could never feel really close to Lon; not really. He was a strange kind of a loner. You could tell what time of day it was by looking at his bottle.

Don't get me wrong. I liked him and I enjoyed working with him. We were good friends and never had an argument all the time we were together. But if he had scenes with a lot of dialogue they'd always do them in the morning. He always could function, but he'd get a little slurry by three in the afternoon. He always looked good and showed up—he was a professional.

He was a good friend of Broderick Crawford and they all drank. I worked on a HIGHWAY PATROL and the guy was drinking a Tom Collins and they'd start coming on a little tray at ten or eleven in the morning and just all through the day. Those guys drank and it killed them all. I used to like to drink, but never ever when I worked. I'd wait until the day was over, especially if I had a lot of dialogue to remember. You just don't dare play with that. That's your living.

Lon was a multifaceted gentleman. He was a great big guy. He was an Olympic wrestling coach for the United States. He was a big, powerful guy, and he loved to hunt and fish, and was a good cook. He was always cooking up duck dinners or Canadian trout dinners. I liked him and I was very sorry that he passed away.

Everybody remembers that his father was the big silent film star who did THE HUNCHBACK OF NOTRE DAME and THE PHANTOM OF THE OPERA and all those things that involved crazy makeup. But if you count the films that Lon Chaney Sr. did, I don't think he did ten big features, but they were major features and he was a big star. Lon must've made fifty pictures and he seemed to have done almost every monster picture ever made back then.

Lon had a very strange upbringing; his father and his mother didn't like him or something. I don't know, but this is what he used to talk about. He was bitterly estranged from them. This was in 1956 when we did this series, and Lon Sr. died in 1930, and we'd go to parties and some 20 year old would come up and say, "I remember your father," and he would just leave at that.

I liked Lon, and I had fun with him, but I never felt that I really knew him.

HAWKEYE was the first filmed television series ever made in Canada, and we had a wonderful pool of actors working out of Toronto, which is the acting center of Canada. I got to know some wonderful people. In fact I got to know my wife up there. She'd gone to the Royal Academy in England and she was just a gorgeous little young gal, and she worked on HAWKEYE. I think we were married in about three weeks.

So that year I spent up there making HAW-KEYE was very satisfying and I enjoyed the job. The schedule was easy. We'd shoot four days to make a half-hour. On THE LONE RANGER, every

one I ever made was shot in two days. And the scripts were a lot longer then. They didn't take out for as much commercial time as they do now. Making THE LONE RANGER was really kind of frantic. The scripts would run maybe 34 pages. Now a half hour runs about 24 pages. And out of that they'd originally try to shoot 16 to 18 pages a day. Today it's unheard of to even shoot ten, and I'd be on damn near every page when I was doing THE LONE RANGER. That was the very early days of television.

YOU WORKED WITH BUST-ER CRABBE?

On some serials and Westerns. I'd known Buster Crabbe from the 1932 Olympics. I was just a young teenager then and a friend of mine was in charge of all the swimming pools and beaches of Los Angeles County. He ran the big swimming stadium where they all worked and he'd sneak me in there when these swimmers from all over the world were working out. Buster was a world champion swimmer in those days. I got to know him and he was older than I was by

about ten years and we got to be kind of friends.

So years later we bump into each other in the picture business. He was a wonderful guy. He bought the first aqualung I ever saw. Cousteau was making them in France, and Buster being a very prominent swimmer, got one. And another actor who's a really good friend of mine, Rick Vallin, and Buster and I would do things together because we were really good friends. Buster got a big kick out of having that.

I still ran into Buster here and there through the years. He ran a swimming program at the New York Athletic Club and I was in New York once for about six months and I could always go down there and go swimming any time I wanted. He was a real gentleman.

Buster got stuck kind of like I did. You'd get stuck making serials and little low-budget pictures and you'd never get a shot at doing anything really good. They didn't think of you as a quality actor. They were afraid to take a chance, I guess. Buster was a good actor, and we used to talk about this. We never got a chance to do anything much with all these pictures we got to work in. I studied at the Playhouse and I could do pages of dialogue in one take usually—I had a good memory. So I worked all the time because I could do all the stunts, I could do all the dialogue in one or two takes. I was a gold mine for them because time was money. But you never got any particularly well-written scripts. It was all rush, rush, rush, hurry, hurry. I think Buster might have been a bigger star, but he was a real nice guy.

WHAT WAS THE FIRST SERIAL YOU WORKED IN?

That was JACK ARMSTRONG, THE ALL-AMERICAN BOY. I'd been in World War Two and came back from Japan. I'd known Jon Hall and Francis Langford quite well. She used to be Bob Hope's singer, and when I was in the service, whenever I was in Los Angeles I'd wind up over at Jon Hall's house. That was another strange guy, but he was a good friend to me. So I got out of the service and he was making a Western at Universal, and he said to c'mon over, because this is what people do. So I got on a pretty good picture with Margaret Lindsay and I was one of the bad guys and so got on salary for five weeks. That was kind of neat.

Then he (Jon Hall) went over to Columbia, to Sam Katzman and got a job on a serial and they were looking for a double, and we were exactly the same size and kind of looked alike. I'd been a worker on cattle ranches when I was a kid and I could ride and do most anything, and I'd also done some boxing. But doing stunts is a whole different world, which I learned very fast. So I got a job

doubling Jon Hall in this one serial for Sam Katzman. And after that Katzman called me back and asked me if I'd like to do JACK ARMSTRONG. So they just gave me the lead in it. I'd had a lot of acting experience. I didn't know it at the time, but that was a very expensive budget for a serial with a five-week shooting schedule. That was a lot of fun to do. I was supposed to be a high school kid but I was actually about 28. But that worked all right. Nobody complained. Five weeks was exceptionally long for a serial to be shot. They usually shot them in three to four weeks. The script looked like the telephone book.

I liked acting. I liked to be acting. I liked the action, the activity. It was fun. I had a pleasant life doing all that stuff.

HOW DID YOU COME TO GET CAST IN THE ROLE OF THE LONE RANGER?

The guy who was producing it in those days was Jack Chertok and he was probably one of the cheapest guys that ever worked in Hollywood. Clayton Moore had done quite a few LONE RANGER's and I'm sure they had some dispute with him. Probably he wanted to get paid. In those days they thought you could wear a mask and you couldn't identify any particular actor. Several other guys had played the Lone Ranger on radio and in serials.

I had worked on THE LONE RANGER as bad guys when Clayton was the Lone Ranger so they knew me and they knew I could do a lot of dialogue and make it believable. I'd done some RED RYDER's with Jim Bannon where I played the bad guy and they screened those and there was a lot of horseback riding and fighting.

And as I say, I worked on horse and cattle ranches when I was a kid and was a good rider. I kind of looked like the comic strip more then Clayton did, and the comic strip was a big deal then. I don't know how many other actors they looked at, but I got the part. They didn't pay me much either. It was unbelievable. But being an out-of-work actor, to have a steady job for awhile is great.

I became very good friends with Jay Silverheels, who played Tonto for both me and Clayton, and what a delightful guy he was. He was a real Mohawk Indian from Brampton, Canada. He'd been a La-Crosse player and he was quite an athlete and just a great guy. He used to have a good time kidding me because I'd have pages and pages of dialogue to wade through every day but he'd come running in with some short message and then I'd talk for two pages. He'd say, "Me go," and then jump on his horse and say, "Get 'em up, Scout" and he'd ride out. He used to stick his head out of his dressing room, watching me bleeding with the dialogue and he'd wave and laugh. We were good friends and it was tragic when he died. I went to see him in the hospital a few days before he died and he didn't weigh 90 pounds, I don't think. He'd had some strokes, but he knew me. Jay was a nice guy.

Doing THE LONE RANGER was a job. They made every one in two days and we didn't get paid worth a damn. I made 52 episodes in 1952. Nowadays a season is considered 24 episodes, or less. But in those days I guess they felt they had to have 52 episodes to be shown over 52 weeks a year. So we cranked them out.

Another odd thing. If you were identified with some kind of popular character in a TV series, they thought that the public just identified you as that character. Poor actors who worked in other series with their bare face hanging out, so to speak, couldn't get another job! After I worked on THE LONE RANGER, I couldn't get another job for a year and a half or so, and I had a mask and a hat. They said, "Oh, no, you were the Lone Ranger." It used to make me so mad, then that wore off and it began to make sense and I worked in a lot of things.

WHAT HAPPENED AT THE END OF THE 52 SHOWS THAT CONVINCED CLAYTON MOORE TO COME BACK?

Clayton was really taken with being the Lone Ranger. He just made a career out of it. They made 39 more in color about three or four years after I made my episodes, and Clayton did those and two features with the Lone Ranger.

And then years and years later they made THE LEGEND OF THE LONE RANGER and they asked Clayton and me to be in it, but he wouldn't be in it. I don't know why. That was a good job for me. I played an old frontier newspaper editor who got hung early in the picture. That was fun, except that the picture died.

WHAT WAS IT LIKE MAKING THAT FILM?

It was a big budget, 20 million dollar picture, and I got a fantastic salary. They said, "Drop everything! Go to Santa Fe!" The next day after I got the part I had to leave. So I flew to Albuquerque and drove up to Santa Fe. I had a nice suite in the Hilton Hotel there and the whole company was still shooting in Arizona. I sat there for about ten days, on salary, getting a per diem, living it up in the hotel. It was wonderful. So finally they came to town and then they fiddled around and fiddled around and I think I worked on the picture for four or five weeks but the actual time of my working was maybe five days but it was spread out. It all goes by sets. When they're ready to shoot on one set they do everything that happens on that one set, regardless of when it takes place in the picture. So that was a neat job. I liked that.

I got to know Bill Fraker, the cameraman/director on that. I've done a lot of camera work, too. I was always a frustrated cameraman. I wound up shooting a picture. I shot tons of stuff for Universal. It was called SLONE. A terrible picture, but I photographed it beautifully. It was a low-budget pot-boiler made in the Phillipines. I don't think it ever saw a theater, but it got out on cassette and made its money back, I guess.

WHO WERE SOME OF YOUR GUEST-STARS ON EPISODES OF THE LONE RANGER?

All the good character people. Pierce Leydon, who was a famous bad guy in a million Westerns. One of the first jobs Lee Van Cleef ever had was as a bad guy on THE LONE RANGER, and he was all depressed about it. He was a young guy then, but boy he had that evil look! He was the baddest-looking guy, but he was actually very nice. He was great. So we were talking one day while we were setting up. I liked the guy and I saw that he really had something. But he was depressed because it's hard to be a struggling actor. If you're not established, you work a little, and then you don't, you work a little, and then you don't. When I was young and doing that I always avoided any kind of responsibilities. I wouldn't even buy a car on time. But if you want to settle down and have some kind of normal life, it's an awful way to go. Nowadays if you get on a series you make so much money you can be rich in a couple of years. But getting back to Lee Van Cleef, I told him, "Lee, you have a wonderful look. You could make a good, steady living all your life playing heavies. Now don't get discouraged. Don't give up. You're going to make it!" Then a few years later he went over to Italy and Spain and just caught fire and became a big star. I hadn't seen him in thirty years or more, and I'm walking out of the Manilla hotel in the Phillipines and I bumped into him. We looked at each other and he knew me, and of course there's no mistaking him. I reminded him of that old conversation and tears came to his eyes. He threw his arms around me. Then he went his way and I went mine and I haven't seen him since. But that was an interesting thing that happened where I encouraged a guy and he became very successful. (NOTE: The day after we conducted this interview, we learned Lee Van Cleef had died.)

Almost all of the prominent character people of the time worked on the show. We didn't use too many girls. It was all horses and bad guys mostly. But a few nice gals came through there that I worked with.

THERE ARE A NUMBER OF ACTORS WHO GUEST-STARRED ON THE LONE RANGER WHO WENT ON TO BECOME VERY WELL-KNOWN, SUCH AS GUY WILLIAMS AND DeFOREST KELLEY.

Deforest Kelley was a good friend of mine, too. I ran into him in the Army. I was a First Sergeant in the Artillery for a couple of years. Then I got transferred to the Air Service Command to do a recruiting thing and I was a First Sergeant there with a giant bunch of responsibilities. So I had to come to Los Angeles for something and I got transferred to the film unit in Culver City at the Hal Roach Studio. Fort Roach, we called it. I was there about a month and made some training films and got to know DeForest Kelley quite well. We became good friends and stayed in touch. That was in World War Two, about 1943. He's a very nice guy with a very nice wife. We were all friends. There was an actress named Phyllis Coates I was going with when I was doing THE LONE RANGER, and we had dinners with DeForest and his wife.

The picture that I met him on was a training film on how to use 50 calibre machine guns. I'd been in the Coast Artillery for several years and they'd sent me to an ordnance

> *"So I walk on the set and here's all these actors making these training films. Not one person on that set knew how to operate a 50 calibre machine gun; how to take it apart and put it together"*

school and so I was an expert on small arms, which was everything up to and including the 50 calibre machine gun. So I walk on the set and here's all these actors making these training films. Not one person on that set knew how to operate a 50 calibre machine gun; how to take it apart and put it together, how it worked. Thank G-d I showed up. So I showed everybody how to do it, and that's how I got to know DeForest. He was one of the actors who was supposed to be doing this. I've got a picture of us someplace from that. I worked with him in other things over the years. I was very happy for him when he got that role on STAR TREK. It's nice to have a running part that lasts.

131

CAN YOU RECALL ANYTHING UNUSUAL THAT HAPPENED ON THE LONE RANGER WHICH WAS CAUSED BY TRYING TO FILM THE SHOW SO QUICKLY?

No, not really. Everybody asks, "Well, did anything funny happen?" Nothing funny happened; it was grim trying to do 16 to 18 pages a day. There was no time for levity or fooling around, not that we didn't tell jokes and do things, but you didn't get too frivolous. So it was just damn serious business to get the thing shot.

We had two directors with their first assistants—Paul Landers and Holly Morse. One director would shoot a picture for two days while the other director and his assistant prepared the next one. So they worked in shifts and they were both really nice guys. They had a sense of humor, so it wasn't unpleasant or anything. When you get on a big picture where there's lots of money you can fool around more, but they didn't waste a second. When they packed up a set and moved, boy, they moved! The minute I wasn't in something, I was in my dressing room trying to memorize the next scene. I used to get up at five in the morning and start memorizing and be at the studio at 7:30.

It was so ridiculous, they put corrective makeup on me so that I looked like the comic strip. You couldn't see my face under the mask! But I could sit in that makeup chair for about a half an hour to forty-five minutes and nobody could talk to me and I could concentrate on my script.

When I started it, one of its creators, George Trendle, believed that one of the keys to its success was that the Lone Ranger was kind of military, and forthright, and he couldn't let us use contractions. You couldn't say couldn't! You'd have to say "could not." I threw that out the window after a few episodes. In spite of the fact that they didn't pay me worth a damn, I've had a lot of fun having been the old Lone Ranger through the years—dining out on it, as they say.

A good part of the crew on THE LONE RANGER liked to go deep sea fishing, and I loved to go. Every two weeks we'd get Saturday and Sunday off, so we'd go out fishing. In one scene once I had this long speech about the Indians going on the warpath and a renegade Indian Chief was doing all this, and I had pages of dialogue telling these Army guys about this bad Indian chief, and it was Chief Yelloweye. And I went on and on, really going at it, and I said, "And the one that's doing this is Yellowtail!" which is a fish! We'd all been fishing for yellowtail. Well, the crew fell apart. That was funny, except that I got to do it all over again. Chief Yellowtail!

YOU MADE APPEARANCES IN RECENT YEARS AS THE LONE RANGER ON HAPPY DAYS AND THE GREATEST AMERICAN HERO?

I did HAPPY DAYS. It was a character's birthday and he'd always wanted to meet the Lone Ranger. It was the 200th HAPPY DAYS or something like that.

Then I did a GREATEST AMERICAN HERO as the Lone Ranger. That was really nice. I had a really good little scene to do. It was for Stephen Cannell and they're a pretty classy operation and treated me very nicely. I had a really nice little part in that which I enjoyed doing.

WERE YOU ESSENTIALLY PLAYING YOURSELF?

Yes. The character was a school teacher, and he took his kids to the shopping center because the Lone Ranger was going to appear there. They hired me to do it and they found my old Lone Ranger suit up at Western Costume or somewhere. Now I'd always reared the horse. I was a cowboy! So they brought a nice white horse out there for me and I was supposed to rear it up and I had all this dialogue and scenes. But these stunt guys had convinced the company that it was dangerous for me to rear the horse, so they hired a guy to double me, and he made a lot of dough, but I didn't know all that. So they told me, "Here's the horse," and I had to sit on him and walk him in. And I said, "Yeah, he's okay. Does he rear pretty good?" and I reared him a couple of times and they said, "Oh, G-d, don't do that!" They didn't want the director to see me rearing the horse. So having been an ex-stuntman I knew the game they were playing, so I let them do it.

What a nice guy William Katt is. I had a nice scene with him. His father was Bill Williams, I think, and his mother was an actress.

So my life in and around Hollywood was always interesting. My best friend was Jackie Coogan, the child star. I met him surfing. I was one of the first guys who ever surfed in California. In the early Thirties, Coogan and I used to go to Malibu when the surf was up real good, and if we weren't working we'd go down there practically every day. At Malibu you can get out real easy there. You just go out a little bit and then you're out past the breaker point and the waves break way out, but you're around them by then. So it's a great place because you don't kill yourself paddling out all the time. We used to surf every day and maybe in a week we'd see four other guys. It was before Fiberglass. I had a red wood and balsa board that was eleven feet long and weighed 96 pounds.

I was born here and grew up here. As I look back, of course you tend to remember the good things. That's human nature. But I had a lot of fun in the picture business. Met lots of interesting people. And of course the Lone Ranger was fun to have done and it's fun to talk about.

> "So my life in and around Hollywood was always interesting. My best friend was Jackie Coogan, the child star. I met him surfing. I was one of the first guys who ever surfed in California."

The Best Known Ranger of All

The Lone Ranger is Clayton Moore; Clayton Moore is the Lone Ranger. Although Clayton Moore hasn't appeared in a new adventure since 1958, his features still come to mind when the name of the masked rider of the plains is evoked.

Moore became synonymous with the hero in the Fifties. Not even a new wide screen version in 1981 could elbow him aside in the hearts and minds of his fans who grew up as he rode the Western plains each week on television. No one will ever become as identified with the character as Moore. He appeared in nearly 200 television episodes and two motion pictures in the role. Even long after the series had been cancelled, Moore continued to make appearances as the Ranger.

135

Born in Chicago on September 14, 1914, Moore began his career in show business as a trapeze artist in a traveling circus. He broke into films playing small roles in B Westerns as both an actor and a stunt man. In 1940 he had a small role in the United Artists film KIT CARSON which starred Jon Hall. But he advanced to the role of leading man in the 1942 serial THE PERILS OF NYOKA playing the male lead opposite Kay Aldridge. (This serial was recently released on tape under its re-release title: NYOKA AND THE TIGERMEN with Moore billed above Aldridge on the packaging.)

When America beckoned in World War II, Moore joined the Air Force and served from 1942 to 1945, interrupting his film career when it was just starting to take off. He resumed his rise upon release from the service, and Moore, unlike such serial stars as Buster Crabbe and Kirk Alyn, did not limit himself to male leads. He was just as likely to play a villain. In THE CRIMSON GHOST (1946), Moore played Ashe, the chief henchman of the title character. Since the Crimson Ghost himself appeared only to send his thugs on assignments, it was Moore who constantly clashed with the film's hero, Charles Quigley. Then in 1947 Moore played the hero in JESSE JAMES RIDES AGAIN. In 1948 he was also the lead in G-MEN NEVER FORGET and THE ADVENTURES OF FRANK AND JESSE JAMES. In early 1949 he starred in THE GHOST OF ZORRO shortly before being signed as The Lone Ranger. Moore had also appeared in a supporting role in SHERIFF OF WICHITA (1949) which was a star vehicle for Allan "Rocky" Lane.

The first three episodes of the new LONE RANGER television series retold the origin in the only continued story the series ever aired. The story reunited Moore with two of his co-stars from PERILS OF NYOKA. Tris Coffin, who had played a villain in that serial, portrayed Captain Reid, the brother of the Texas Ranger who would soon don a mask to fight for law and order in the early West, while George J. Lewis, who played good guys as frequently as bad guys in films, was the traitorous guide, Collins, who led the six Texas Rangers into a trap, fell to his death at the conclusion of part two of the three-part origin story. Lewis had his most prominent role as the venerable father of Don Diego in the late Fifties television series ZORRO.

Following his making the first 78 episodes of THE LONE RANGER in 1949 and 1950 (which ran on television until September 1952), Moore requested a raise, which producer George W. Trendle refused. Rebuffed, Moore took the only action he felt honor would allow. He quit and returned to doing features and serials until rehired to play the Lone Ranger again in 1954. During his time away from the series, Moore's got worse parts than he had been playing prior to signing on as the Ranger in '49. The films were not as well written even though his roles were just as substantial. In 1952 he played the chief henchman in Republic's RADAR MEN FROM THE MOON, a role virtually identical to what he had played in THE CRIMSON GHOST. Also in 1952 he starred as the long-haired Buffalo Bill in BUFFALO BILL IN TOMAHAWK TERRITORY, a standard B Western. For serials he

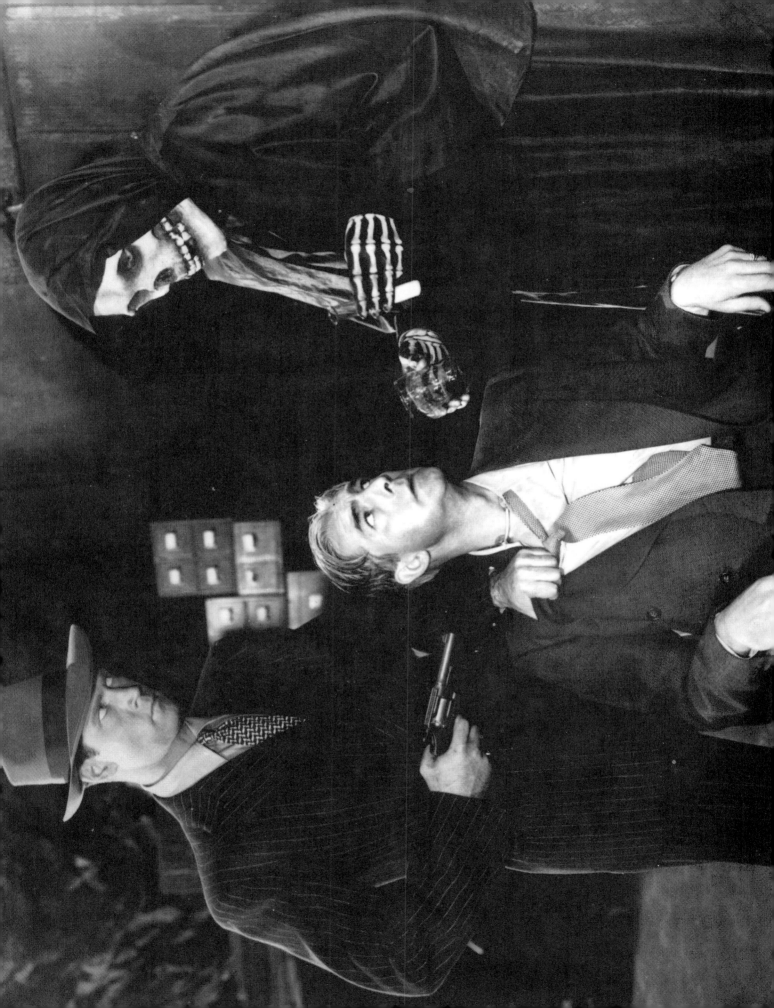

starred in SON OF GERONIMO (Columbia, 1953), JUNGLE DRUMS OF AFRICA (Republic, 1953) and GUNFIGHTERS OF THE NORTHWEST (Columbia, 1954). He also played supporting roles in films such as the 1953 Rex Allen Western DOWN LAREDO WAY. He even played a heavy on an episode of the HOPALONG CASSIDY television series. No doubt fans seeing that face and hearing that distinctive voice coming from the wrong side of the law must have been surprised indeed.

In Moore's absence, John Hart stood in as the Lone Ranger for 52 episodes filmed one after the other and aired from September 1952 until 1954. Hart was tired of the role by the time he finished shooting those episodes and not sorry at all they didn't call him back when the series went into production. He said as much in a TV GUIDE article in the June 30, 1956. The article also showed photos of all the actors who had played the Lone Ranger, including one of Clayton Moore from PERILS OF NYOKA (so much for keeping the Masked Man's face a secret).

From 1954 through 1956, new episode of THE LONE RANGER were produced, with shooting of the final 39 in color. By this time the Jack Wrather Corporation had purchased the rights to the Lone Ranger and other properties from George W. Trendle and Wrather decided to make his investment pay off quickly by producing a feature film.

The opulent THE LONE RANGER (1956) was dramatic and heroic without being silly. Although the plot of whites masquerading as Indians to stir up trouble was old hat, the story had enough twists and exciting touches to elevate it above the commonplace. It holds up well 35 years later. It's sequel, THE LONE RANGER AND THE LOST CITY OF GOLD (1958), while entertaining, lacks the ambition displayed by the first feature. This film would mark the last time Moore donned the garb of the Lone Ranger on the screen other than in cameo appearances and commercials, and these proved few and far between.

Although Moore did not enter an agreement with his former employers, the Wrather Corporation, the actor continued to make personal appearances over the years dressed as the Lone Ranger. The Wrather Corporation looked the other way until they chose to bring the Lone Ranger back to the screen with another actor in the part. Then, in late 1979, they instructed Moore to cease appearing in public in the trademark mask. Moore took the Wrather Corporation to court and lost, but he satisfied the court's restraining order by wearing a large pair of wraparound sunglasses which were the same size as his old mask. Headlines across the country proclaimed that the Lone Ranger could no longer don his mask, and generated a lot of bad press for the new motion picture. Moore was interviewed on radio and television shows across the country, climaxing in an appearance on the then popular REAL PEOPLE.

In 1985, following the death of Jack Wrather, the Wrather Corporation quietly lifted their restraining order against Moore. Once again he would be allowed to wear the Lone familiar mask in public without restrictions.

"I'm extremely happy and pleased for my fans," Moore said. "I will continue wearing the white hat and black mask until I ride up into the big ranch in the sky."

Fate wasn't about to let the Lone Ranger (that is, Clayton Moore) get away that easy without a little more excitement. In 1987, while Moore was traveling for a personal appearance, he had checked his twin Colt .45 pistols and holster through in baggage. They were stolen by a Houston baggage handler who was later arrested, placed on 10 years probation and fined $5,000. The collector who had unwittingly bought the pistols from the baggage handler for $200 brought them forward and turned them over to police as soon as he learned of the theft. Then in 1988, while Moore was in Spartanburg, South Carolina appearing in a fire safety program for children he came upon a hit-and-run accident on the way back to his motel. Moore saw an injured motorcyclist and emerged from his car to assist the man until an ambulance could arrive. Dressed in his mask and Western outfit, he directed traffic and assisted emergency personnel. The injured man said that Moore promised to give him a silver bullet as a memento of the incident.

Moore most recently appeared on screen as the host of the Rhino Video releases of the LONE RANGER TV episodes (two per tape). Wearing sunglasses rather than a mask, he sits in a chair on a set, stiffly reading cue cards which describe the episode about to be shown. His delivery indicates he's reading the words for the first time without benefit of retakes. He looks ill and sounds like he has a cold. Fans who anxiously anticipated seeing Moore on these tapes have expressed shock at his appearance. The tapes have the bold announcement: ALL NEW INTRODUCTIONS AND LONE RANGER TRIVIA HOSTED BY CLAYTON MOORE! Yet the introductions are but a few seconds long before the camera cuts away and then cuts back to Moore once more stiffly reading cue cards giving some piece of trivia such as what "kemo sabe" means or where the Lone Ranger gets his silver from. His one sentence answers fail to excite and those who expect an interview are sorely disappointed. For all Moore does on these tapes they might just as well have dressed anyone as the Lone Ranger and had him read the cue cards. The tapes themselves are of excellent quality with beautiful full color publicity stills of Moore as the Lone Ranger on the box. They are also being released on Laser Disc. (For more information contact Rhino Video, 2225 Colorado Ave., Santa Monica, CA 90404.) The tapes have received low distribution and are difficult to find even in stores specializing in classic videos of films and old television shows.

Moore has consistently refused interviews for over a decade. Reportedly Moore is working with another writer on his own biography, but nearly fifteen years have passed since this was first rumored.

In 1980, Bob Raggi met Moore in New York City and had some casual conversations with him which he turned into an article published in FAVORITE WESTERNS & SERIALS PLUS #21 (Spring 1985). In that piece Raggi remarks that, "He talked vaguely of writing a book on his experiences and claimed the tight schedule of appearances he was on gave him little free time."

At the time Raggi met Moore, the actor was still in bitter contention with the Wrather Corporation over his right to wear the mask and would talk of little else. Moore was interviewed on radio station WOR by Patricia McCann, and Raggi writes, "I was somewhat saddened at the results of the interview. McCann gave Clay a good opportunity to expound on many areas of the long running T.V. series, but he kept turning the conversation back to the mask." Moore even admitted to Raggi that he had turned down $150,000 to endorse the then forthcoming LEGEND OF THE LONE RANGER, stating, "Bob, I wouldn't do it for a million." When Raggi suggested it would have been nice if the film had shown Moore turning the mask over to a younger Ranger, Moore rejected the idea out of hand, stating, "Why? They've got the real Lone Ranger right here." But a year later Moore had apparently had a change of heart.

In a story published in The Los Angeles Times for May 24, 1981 (the week the new film was released), Moore stated his own idea for the movie they should've done. "Tonto dies and I find a young man who is on the fence between going bad and standing for what is right and just. There's a lot of good in him but it needs to be developed. I take him under my wing and we fight the forces of evil together. At the end of the film, after he's proven himself, I give him my silver bullets and, with my back to the camera, I take off the mask and hand it to him. I advise him to seek a faithful companion to help him in his work and tell him the task of seeking justice is now his. I ride off into the sunset and the new Lone Ranger says, 'Hi Yo Silver, away' as the 'William Tell' overture wells up. It would have been beautiful," said Moore.

Ten years after THE LEGEND OF THE LONE RANGER was filmed, discussions are now underway regarding a new theatrical feature. There's even a new LONE RANGER TV series in the works, scheduled to appear in syndication in the fall of 1990 (although a call to Paladium Entertainment in New York indicated that the show had not yet been cast and wouldn't go into production until at least May of '90). It's doubtful that Moore would be involved in either of these projects although we can expect his voice to be heard.

As long as television fans remember the refrain, "Hi-yo Silver!," Clayton Moore will never be forgotten.

Moore continues to make personal appearances as the Lone Ranger as he approaches his 76th birthday, and has said that he'll continue acting the role in public life "as long as they could strap me in the saddle."

THE COUCH POTATO BOOK CATALOG 5715 N BALSAM, LAS VEGAS, NV 89130

THE ILLUSTRATED STEPHEN KING

A complee guide to the novels and short stories of Stephen King illustrated by Steve Bissette and others...$12.95

GUNSMOKE YEARS

The definitive book of America's most successful television series. 22 years of episode guide, character profiles, interviews and more...240 pages, $14.95

THE KING COMIC HEROES

The complete story of the King Features heroes including Prince Valiant, Flash Gordon, Mandrake, The Phantom, Secret Agent, Rip Kirby, Buz Sawyer, Johnny Hazard and Jungle Jim. These fabulous heroes not only appeared in comic strips and comic books but also in movies and serials, Includes interviews with Hal Foster, Al Williamson and Lee Falk...$14.95

Special discounts are available for library, school, club or other bulk orders. Please inquire.

IF YOUR FAVORITE TELEVISION SERIES ISN'T HERE, LET US KNOW...
AND THEN STAY TUNED!

And always remember that if every world leader was a couch potato and watched TV 25 hours a day, 8 days a week, there would be no war...

THE COUCH POTATO BOOK CATALOG 5715 N BALSAM, LAS VEGAS, NV   89130

TREK YEAR 1
The earliest voyages and the creation of the series. An in-depth episode guide, a look at the pilots, interviews, character profiles and more... 160 pages...$10.95

TREK YEAR 2
TREK YEAR 3
$12.95 each

THE ANIMATED TREK
Complete in one volume $14.95

THE MOVIES
The chronicle of all the movies... 116 pages...$12.95

STAR TREK

THE LOST YEARS
For the first time anywhere, the exclusive story of the Star Trek series that almost was including a look at every proposed adventure and an interview with the man that would have replaced Spock. Based on interviews and exclusive research... 160 pages...$14.95

NEXT GENERATION
Complete background of the new series. Complete first season including character profiles and actor biographies...160 pages ...$19.95

THE TREK ENCYCLOPEDIA
The reference work to Star Trek including complete information on every character, alien race and monster that ever appeared as well as full information on every single person that ever worked on the series from the stars to the stunt doubles from extras to producers, directors, make-up men and cameramen...**over 360 pages. UPDATED EDITION. Now includes planets, ships and devices**...$19.95

INTERVIEWS ABOARD THE ENTERPRISE
Interviews with the cast and crew of Star Trek and the Next Generation. From Eddie Murphy to Leonard Nimoy and from Jonathan Frakes to Marina Sirtis. Over 100 pages of your favorites. $18.95

THE ULTIMATE TREK
The most spectacular book we have ever offered. This volume completely covers every year of Star Trek, every animated episode and every single movie. Plus biographies, interviews, profiles, and more. Over 560 pages! Hardcover only. Only a few of these left. $75.00

TREK HANDBOOK and TREK UNIVERSE
The Handbook offers a complete guide to conventions, clubs, fanzines.
The Universe presents a complete guide to every book, comic, record and everything else.
Both volumes are edited by Enterprise Incidents editor James Van Hise. Join a universe of Trek fun!
Handbook...$12.95   Universe...$17.95

THE CREW BOOK
The crew of the Enterprise including coverage of Kirk, Spock, McCoy, Scotty, Uhura, Chekov, Sulu and all the others...plus starship staffing practices...250 pages...$17.95

THE MAKING OF THE NEXT GENERATION: SCRIPT TO SCREEN
THIS BOOK WILL NOT BE PRINTED UNTIL APRIL OR MAY. Analysis of every episode in each stage, from initial draft to final filmed script. Includes interviews with the writers and directors. 240 pages...$14.95

Boring, but Necessary Ordering Information!

Payment: All orders must be prepaid by check or money order. Do not send cash. All payments must be made in US funds only.

Shipping: We offer several methods of shipment for our product.

Postage is as follows:

For books priced under $10.00— for the first book add $2.50. For each additional book under $10.00 add $1.00. (This is per individual book priced under $10.00, not the order total.)

For books priced over $10.00— for the first book add $3.25. For each additional book over $10.00 add $2.00. (This is per individual book priced over $10.00, not the order total.)

These orders are filled as quickly as possible. Sometimes a book can be delayed if we are temporarily out of stock. You should note on your order whether you prefer us to ship the book as soon as available or send you a merchandise credit good for other TV goodies or send you your money back immediately. Shipments normally take 2 or 3 weeks, but allow up to 12 weeks for delivery.

Special UPS 2 Day Blue Label RUSH SERVICE: Special service is available for desperate Couch Potatos. These books are shipped within 24 hours of when we receive your order and should take 2 days to get from us to you.

For the first **RUSH SERVICE** book under $10.00 add $4.00. For each additional 1 book under $10.00 and $1.25. (This is per individual book priced under $10.00, not the order total.)

For the first **RUSH SERVICE** book over $10.00 add $6.00. For each additional book over $10.00 add $3.50 per book. (This is per individual book priced over $10.00, not the order total.)

Canadian and Foreign shipping rates are the same except that Blue Label RUSH SERVICE is not available. All Canadian and Foreign orders are shipped as books or printed matter.

DISCOUNTS! DISCOUNTS! Because your orders are what keep us in business we offer a discount to people that buy a lot of our books as our way of saying thanks. On orders over $25.00 we give a 5% discount. On orders over $50.00 we give a 10% discount. On orders over $100.00 we give a 15% discount. On orders over $150.00 we give a 20% discount. Please list alternates when possible. Please state if you wish a refund or for us to backorder an item if it is not in stock.

100% satisfaction guaranteed. We value your support. You will receive a full refund as long as the copy of the book you are not happy with is received back by us in reasonable condition. No questions asked, except we would like to know how we failed you. Refunds and credits are given as soon as we receive back the item you do not want.

Please have mercy on Phyllis and carefully fill out this form in the neatest way you can. Remember, she has to read a lot of them every day and she wants to get it right and keep you happy! You may use a duplicate of this order blank as long as it is clear. **Please don't forget to include payment! And remember, we** *love* **repeat friends...**

▪▪▪▪▪▪▪▪▪▪▪▪▪▪▪▪▪▪▪▪▪▪▪▪▪▪ ORDER FORM ▪▪▪▪▪▪▪▪▪▪▪▪▪▪▪▪▪▪▪▪▪▪▪▪▪▪▪▪▪

_____ The Phantom $16.95
_____ The Green Hornet $16.95
_____ The Shadow $16.95
_____ Flash Gordon Part One $16.95 _____ Part Two $16.95
_____ Blackhawk $16.95
_____ Batman $16.95
_____ The UNCLE Technical Manual One $9.95 _____ Two $9.95
_____ The Green Hornet Television Book $14.95
_____ Number Six The Prisoner Book $14.95
_____ The Wild Wild West $17.95
_____ Trek Year One $10.95
_____ Trek Year Two $12.95
_____ Trek Year Three $12.95
_____ The Animated Trek $14.95
_____ The Movies $12.95
_____ Next Generation $19.95
_____ The Lost Years $14.95
_____ The Trek Encyclopedia $19.95
_____ Interviews Aboard The Enterprise $18.95
_____ The Ultimate Trek $75.00
_____ Trek Handbook $12.95 _____ Trek Universe $17.95
_____ The Crew Book $17.95
_____ The Making of the Next Generation $14.95
_____ The Freddy Krueger Story $14.95
_____ The Aliens Story $14.95
_____ Robocop $16.95
_____ Monsterland's Horror in the '80s $17.95
_____ The Compleat Lost in Space $17.95
_____ Lost in Space Tribute Book $9.95
_____ Lost in Space Tech Manual $9.95
_____ Supermarionation $17.95
_____ The Unofficial Beauty and the Beast $14.95
_____ Dark Shadows Tribute Book $14.95
_____ Dark Shadows Interview Book $18.95
_____ Doctor Who Baker Years $19.95
_____ The Doctor Who Encyclopedia:The 4th Doctor $19.95
_____ Illustrated Stephen King $12.95
_____ Gunsmoke Years $14.95

NAME:_____

STREET:_____

CITY:_____

STATE:_____

ZIP:_____

TOTAL:_____ SHIPPING_____

SEND TO: COUCH POTATO, INC.
5715 N BALSAM, LAS VEGAS, NV 89130